Terri O's
Easy Embellishing

Instantly Accessorize Everyday Objects

Suzanne Chase & Terri O

Sterling Publishing Co., Inc.
New York

Projects designed by Suzanne Chase, Sue Zimmerman, and Terri O.

Photography by Jerry Zimmerman.

Book design by Judy Morgan.

To find out more about Treasure Tape™, visit www.treasuretape.com

Library of Congress Cataloging-in-Publication Data

10 9 8 7 6 5 4 3 2

O, Terri.
  Terri O's easy embellishing : instantly accessorize everyday objects / Suzanne Chase & Terri O.
    p. cm.
  Includes index.
  ISBN-13: 978-1-4027-2487-9
  ISBN-10: 1-4027-2487-X
  1. Textile crafts. 2. Decoration and ornament. 3. Clothing and dress. 4. House furnishings.
  I. Title: Easy embellishing. II. Chase, Suzanne. III. Title.
  TT699.O2 2006
  746--dc22

2005033889

Published by Sterling Publishing Co., Inc.
387 Park Avenue South, New York, NY 10016
©2006 by Suzanne Chase and Terri Ouellette
Distributed in Canada by Sterling Publishing
℅ Canadian Manda Group, 165 Dufferin Street
Toronto, Ontario, Canada M6K 3H6
Distributed in the United Kingdom by GMC Distribution Services
Castle Place, 166 High Street, Lewes, East Sussex, England BN7 1XU
Distributed in Australia by Capricorn Link (Australia) Pty. Ltd.
P.O. Box 704, Windsor, NSW 2756, Australia

Sterling ISBN 13: 978-1-4027-2487-9
ISBN 10: 1-4027-2487-X

For information about custom editions, special sales, premium and
corporate purchases, please contact Sterling Special Sales
Department at 800-805-5489 or specialsales@sterlingpub.com.

Contents

Preface

I have been creative all my life. When I was a little girl, I used to take shoeboxes and make miniature dollhouses out of them, complete with wallpaper and furniture. I used to make my own fake fingernails out of white glue, and I used to decoupage old greeting cards onto wood plaques. I would spend hours alone, cutting, gluing, and painting. In the old days we called it imagination. As I grew, so did my imagination and my interest in creativity.

As I walked the aisles of the craft and hobby show one day, a few years ago, something spectacular caught my eye: an old jeans jacket, decorated as though it should be in a museum! I screamed with excitement and lo and behold, out came Suzanne Chase and Sue Zimmerman, the designers. At that very moment I knew that these two gals were just like me. We all screamed, jumped up and down, and talked at the same time. A relationship was born!

This book is a result of passion: the passion to make anything and everything around you beautiful. Suzanne Chase and Sue Zimmerman, my two new girlfriends, have pioneered a way to make embellishing quick and easy. We are all on the go. If you are at all like us—busy with the kids, hubby, and work, but having a need to create that won't quit—you will have a ball with this book. All the projects were created so that you can express who you are for all to see. You can do the projects quickly and without much expense. Thanks to red-liner tape, you can change your designs as often as you change your mind. So have fun and let the creative energy flow.

—Terri O

Introduction

Your personal style is communicated not only by the clothing you wear, but also by the everyday objects that surround you. This book shows you how to take these common objects, potential communicators of who you are or how you are feeling, and instantly decorate them to express yourself. "Instantly" is key. Time has become a luxury. However, even as our lives get busier and busier, many of us still get that itch to create. So while a lucky few continue to find the time and patience to do traditional forms of crafting like quilting, embroidery, and beadwork, most of us are seeking a quicker fix, a faster way to express our creativity within the reality of our busy lives. Our mission in writing a book that uses red-liner tape was to offer that quick fix. Red-liner tape is super sticky, super strong (industrial strength) and double-sided, so it is a quick and easy alternative to gluing, sewing, and beading. In fact, most projects can be completed in just one sitting. It's also somewhat foolproof, so you don't have to be particularly talented or skilled to create something impressive looking. We (Suzanne Chase and Sue Zimmerman) market our own brand of red-liner tape called Treasure Tape™, but there are other red-liner tapes on the market also, which you can use.

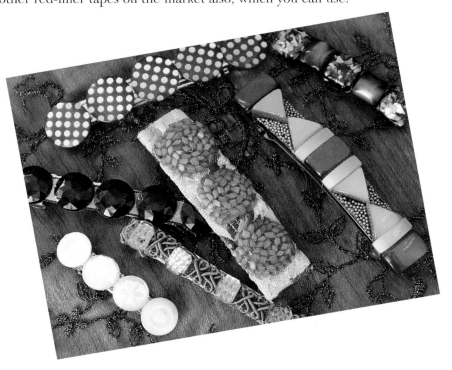

Red-liner tape is not as strong as a glue gun or needlework, but its benefits seem to far outweigh its limitations. Embellishments attached with red-liner tape can be temporary (lasting days, weeks, months, or even years, depending on usage and care), but by the time an item needs to be jazzed up again, you'll probably welcome the opportunity to come up with a new look, especially since embellishing only takes minutes to do.

The first part of the book provides you with information on red-liner tape. It also reviews a wide spectrum of embellishments and other supplies that are perfect for tape crafting.

Next, step-by-step photos and instructions for various tape techniques get your creative juices flowing. A wide range of projects show you how to decorate clothing, handbags, shoes, backpacks, picture frames, looseleaf binders, and more. There's even a special section of wedding projects.

A key for each project lets you know the time needed to complete it, the techniques needed, and the difficulty level. Feel free to use the ideas and techniques offered in this book in new ways to create your own project ideas. In addition to traditional project instructions, Terri O has added her own thoughts and inspirations throughout the book.

—*Suzanne Chase*

Left to right: Terri O works with ribbon as Sue Zimmerman and Suzanne Chase look on.

THE
Basics & Beyond

1 A finished cell phone with faux jewels added on.

Turn ordinary objects into cool personal expressions by instantly embellishing them with all kinds of goodies, using double-sided industrial-strength red-liner tape (photo 1).

✳ Simply stick tape on the object you want to decorate and then embellish it with items that have a flat back, so they will adhere firmly to the tape. Although embellishing with red-liner tape is simple and straightforward, the results are anything but. Each piece you create will be uniquely expressive because of the types of embellishment you choose, how you arrange them, and what you decide to decorate.

✳ Adhere double-sided tape by applying it directly onto the item you want to embellish (photo 2). Run your fingertips over the taped surface to smooth it out. Then simply peel back the top liner to expose the sticky tape.

✳ Apply embellishments of your choice to the exposed tape by gently pressing them into place. When you are pleased with your design, you can place the embellished item in a shallow pan and pour Diamond Beadlets® (our own brand of clear glass microbeads) or other small, granular embellishments such as tiny beads, colored sand, or glitter over the remaining exposed tape (photo 3). Swirl the little beads with fingertips to fully cover the tape. Press them in place. Tap the item on its side to dislodge any loose beads.

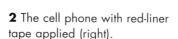

2 The cell phone with red-liner tape applied (right).

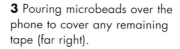

3 Pouring microbeads over the phone to cover any remaining tape (far right).

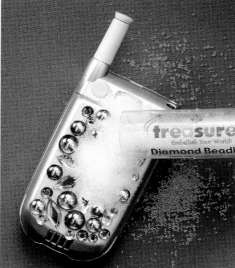

Here is some basic information for working with red-liner tape:

✳ Red-liner tape is the strongest craft tape available. It is perfect for crafting, decorating, and making quick-fix repairs.

✳ It provides an instant, permanent bond to almost any surface, including glass, plastic, metal, leather, wood, paper, fabric, and wax, with strongest bond after 24 hours.

✳ The tape dots and sheets are protected by two liners: a paper backing and a red plastic top liner (photo 4). Rolls of tape have the top liner only. The tape itself is very thin, like plastic wrap (photo 5), and is invisible when applied. It comes in a variety of formats, including sheets, rolls of varying widths, and die-cut shapes. The tape is nontoxic and photo-safe.

✳ The different tape formats are designed for different crafting and decorating jobs (photo 6). Tape rolls are used primarily for trimming and bonding jobs, while tape sheets are best for covering large surface areas and embellishing images. The sheets can be trimmed to size, when necessary, with a standard paper cutter or scissors. Teflon-coated scissors are highly recommended (to avoid adhesive buildup), but regular scissors can also be used, as long as you have an adhesive remover on hand to clean them.

Here are some helpful application tips for crafting with red-liner tape:

✳ Always work on a clean, dry surface.

✳ Clean hands before working with red-liner tape, so skin oils, etc. don't adhere to tape.

✳ Reuse the tape's top protective liner to cover up one area while working on another area.

✳ Always apply larger embellishments first, and fill in remaining exposed tape with microbeads, glitter, etc.

4 When you peel back the top red liner, you expose the clear, sticky tape underneath.

5 Red-liner tape is paper thin and 100% transparent.

6 The tape comes in a variety of convenient formats, including sheets, rolls, and die-cut shapes.

SOURCES OF EMBELLISHMENTS

If you are crafty at all, you will most likely have a cache of embellishments at home, "stuff" you have collected along the way. Even if you are not a big spender with an infamous hoard of goodies, there are plenty of items around the house that are perfect for red-liner crafting. Now is the time to take out all those cool goodies and use them, instead of trying to figure out how to keep them organized. With red-liner tape crafting, anything goes, as long as the embellishment has a flat back or is very small (e.g., microbeads, glitter, sand) so that it adheres well to the tape.

The looks you create can vary dramatically, depending on the embellishments you choose. You can go frilly one day and vintage the next. When you get tired of one look, simply pull the tape off the item and decorate with different embellishments. We have included dozens of embellishment ideas to get your creative juices flowing.

1 Confetti (top, right).

2 Ribbons in an assortment of patterns and widths. Both wired and unwired work well (top, far right).

3 Metallic embroidery threads (bottom, right).

4 Assorted flat-sided beads (bottom, far right).

Scrapbooking and Other Paper Crafts

If you scrapbook, now is the time to pull out your pile of supplies and to consider your loot in a new light. Scrapbooking supplies can be used well beyond the page, so stop trying to organize your overflowing supply chest; start using your supplies to embellish your world. Don't forget all those leftover odds and ends. If you aren't a scrapbooker, you can still take advantage of the incredible array of products that are marketed for this hobby, since most of the supplies are perfect for red-liner tape crafting.

In addition to scrapbooking supplies, there are paper-craft supplies for card-making, quilling, and rubber stamping that you can also add to your designs.

5 Themed woven labels, originally for scrapbooking.

Needle Arts

Anyone with a passion for sewing, quilting, knitting, or embroidery should have a great cache of odds and ends to use for embellishing with red-liner tape. "Stringy stuff" such as ribbons, trim, yarn, and braid are our favorites as they are very forgiving to use. You can easily pull them off the tape to reapply when necessary. Buttons and appliqués are also great embellishments, since they come in so many materials, colors, and styles. If you want to use a button with a shank, you can remove it with a shank remover, a tool sold in the scrapbooking aisle of your local craft store.

6 Unusual button shapes (far left).

7 Fabric appliqués (left).

8 Silk flowers.

Artificial Flowers

You can incorporate all kinds of faux flowers into your designs. Traditional silk flowers can be used, simply by pulling the flowers off the stem and adhering them to the tape. If you are lucky, you will find silk flowers at tag sales and thrift stores for pennies. In addition to silk flowers on stems, you can find all kinds of mulberry-paper flowers and pressed flowers, off of the stem, located in card-making and scrapbooking aisles of craft stores.

Beading and Jewelry Making

Anyone we've met who is into beading is sure to have a significant hoard of beads in all shapes, colors, and sizes, since a large part of creating beautiful beaded jewelry is hunting for great-looking beads. Very small beads, such as seed or bugle beads, work well with red-liner tape, since they are small enough to adhere even though they lack a flat back. Also, there are plenty of large beads on the market, including square and rectangular beads, with a flat side that will adhere securely to the tape. Consider any kind of inexpensive cabochon (unfaceted convex hemispherical or oval-shaped stone or faux stone) or rhinestone—in fact, any flat-backed embellishment designed for a bezel. Rhinestones are the most common; they can be found in most craft stores. Swarovski makes truly beautiful glass beads and rhinestones, which cost more but are wonderful to use for really special accessories. Other supplies can be found by hunting around the house and at tag sales for old costume jewelry or kids' jewelry.

9 Acrylic and glass rhinestones and other decorations (right).

10 Lucite and glass jewelry supplies (far right).

Mosaics

Like faux jewels, mosaic tiles (including glass or plastic tiles and mirror tiles) are excellent for tape crafting because they are designed with a flat back. Due to the popularity of mosaic making, the breadth of tile choices has grown dramatically. When possible, use lightweight tiles of plastic, thin glass, or ceramic, to ensure the best adhesion.

Kids' Stuff

If you have children, especially girls, then you probably will have all kinds of odds and ends for crafting. The first place to look is in all those half-used craft activity kits lying around the house. They frequently contain assorted embroidery floss, confetti, rhinestones, polymer clay beads, glitter, gimp, metal charms, and colored sand. In addition, your child's dress-up bin is a great source for sequined trim, feathers, tulle, ribbons, and costume jewelry. Don't forget to consider family board games, especially the ones no longer in use or with pieces missing, for clever embellishment ideas. Think creatively as you look around your house; even simple kite string can be added to your design. Note: Before snagging supplies this way, remember to check with your child to be sure you are not taking something she cares about keeping.

11 Playing cards and game pieces.

12 Tiles and other pieces from games (far left).

13 Feathers (left).

Home Decorating Supplies

If you have stacks of swatches and trim samples from a time when you bought a new house or decided to redecorate a room, now is the time to take all those goodies out and look at them in a new light. Couch and curtain fabrics, whether swatches or leftover yardage, can be used to create wonderful accessories and gifts. In addition to what you may have tucked away, consider home decorating items you are ready to part with, such as old curtains, old throw pillows, and even old upholstered furniture, since oftentimes they will have a fabulous trim, tassel, or decorative button that can be recycled into your designs. Potential tag-sale items should be scrutinized before discarding, since their decorative details may be of value to you even if the entire item is not.

14 Tassels and trims.

15 Fabric swatches and remnants.

Old Clothing and Accessories

Your own thrift store pile is a great source for buttons, denim, other fabrics, and trims to recycle. In addition, consider the spare buttons you sometimes get in a little packet when you purchase a garment. You may have accumulated a sizeable collection of these handsome, one-of-a-kind buttons. Neckties are another great item to use for embellishing. Most of us have someone in our life who has ties in the closet that he rarely wears. With gentle encouragement, he may be willing and ready to part with them.

16 Ties. Reconsider your items slated for the thrift shop.

Family Keepsakes

Many of you have older family members who have given you their memorabilia to keep as part of the family's history. Some may be items that are off limits because of their emotional or financial value. However, there are usually many other things like old lace, cloth doilies and napkins, buttons, old watch fobs, and other materials from yesteryear that can be used as embellishments to create wonderful vintage style accessories. For those of you who do not have family memorabilia but like the vintage look, there are plenty of ways to purchase vintage style goodies through the Internet as well as at local antique stores, thrift shops, or quilt shows.

17 Old lace, buttons, and ribbon.

Travel Memorabilia

When traveling, you may be inspired to gather and bring home a variety of collectibles, including shells, ticket stubs, and foreign money. These items can be used as embellishments to create functional keepsakes, perhaps incorporated into a picture frame for your desk at the office or used to embellish a pair of slip-on sandals.

Granular Embellishments

Once you have finished embellishing your object with all sorts of goodies, there may be remaining areas of exposed tape that will need to be covered, unless you have chosen to cover your object entirely with ribbon, paper, etc. To cover up the remaining sticky areas, there are many granular embellishments that can be used. The idea is to use something that can be poured over the object to fill in all the nooks and crannies. Some examples are glitter (from ultra fine to chunky), foil flecks for papermaking, and sparkly colored sand. You can also mix these items together to create different effects. Don't forget to bring some sand home from the beach next time you go, since it is a beautiful granular filler when mixed with chunky, iridescent glitter. You will need to make sure it is dry, so leave it out in the sun for a few days, or better yet, microwave it!

18 Shells from beach vacations.

19 Microbeads, glitter, colored sand, and foil flecks all adhere beautifully to the tape and provide a variety of effects.

Here is a list of sources of images to spark your imagination:

✤ Children's and adults' book covers and illustrations

✤ Wall or desk calendars

✤ Playbill covers

✤ Posters

✤ Birth announcements

✤ Magazine covers and clippings

✤ Rubber-stamp images

✤ Needlepoint patterns

✤ Playing cards

✤ Stickers

✤ Fabric patterns

✤ Wedding announcements

✤ Rub-on transfers

✤ Kids' artwork (or yours)

✤ Store-bought cards

✤ Wrapping paper designs

✤ Memorabilia (movie tickets, etc.)

✤ Images from art books

✤ Scrapbooking papers

✤ Ephemeral images and collaged papers

✤ Die-cut paper images

✤ Photos

Images

One of our favorite red-liner tape techniques, Enhancing Images (found on p. 30, in the Techniques section), uses an image which is then covered with double-sided tape and embellished. The image can come from anywhere, especially if you have a color copier or have access to one, enabling you to conserve the original and to size the copy to your liking. If your image is too large or cumbersome to make a color copy, you can perhaps take a digital picture of it and use the print as your image.

20 Stickers, decals, note cards, and other images.

HELPFUL TOOLS

Crafting with red-liner tape is so simple and straightforward that it does not require much special equipment or many skills to get started. Below we describe some helpful tools, which you may already have on hand from your other craft interests, and we list things around the house that you can use as perfect substitutes.

Craft Tray. This tray, or a shallow pan or container of some kind, is needed for the beading step of projects, so that the granular embellishments you pour over the item can be contained. There are a number of craft trays on the market, designed for beading, that have a nice pour-spout for returning unused beads or sand to a storage container. If you do not own one of these, you can use all sorts of other containers, such as a shallow baking pan, a disposable roasting tin, plastic food storage containers, a shirt box, etc. We find paper items (a plate, sheet of paper, or a box) the best choice when working with glitter, since it tends to cling to plastic.

Nonstick Scissors and Adhesive Remover. Nonstick scissors are essential if you want to do a lot of tape crafting. Their protective Teflon coating greatly reduces the amount of adhesive buildup on your scissors. However, if you do not own a pair, you can use regular craft scissors, as long as you have an adhesive remover or oil-free nail-polish remover on hand so that you can clean them frequently.

Paper Cutter. A paper cutter allows you to trim images, as well as sheets of tape, to size. Please note that a ruler and scissors can be used if you do not own a paper cutter, although accuracy is a bit more difficult to achieve.

Craft Knife. A craft knife such as an X-Acto knife is helpful when you need to tape something that is oddly shaped, since it will help you trim away excess tape.

1 Some basic tools include adhesive remover, a craft tray, a craft knife, an awl, bent-nosed tweezers, a shank remover, scissors, and a small brayer.

Bent-Nosed Tweezers. This tool is great for helping you press embellishments, especially threads and other thin fibers, into the tape to secure them. If you don't own a pair, you can purchase one at your local drugstore. You have numerous other choices, such as an awl, a wooden skewer, and a craft stick to handle the same job, but tweezers are particularly good since you can pick up small embellishments with them as well.

Brayer. This small roller with a handle is sold in crafts and art stores, and is helpful for tape crafting when you need to smooth out a sheet of tape that has been applied to a large, flat surface (such as a notebook cover, laptop, or image). If you don't have a brayer, a credit card or the heel of your hand will do the trick.

Tea Strainer. If you find that your microbeads are getting "contaminated" with other, larger embellishments, like seed beads or gold foil, you can use a tea strainer or other fine sieve to separate them.

Shank Remover. Sold as a scrapbooking supply, a shank remover allows you to remove the shank from the back of a button. This lets you use all sorts of buttons (not just the ones with the holes in them) for tape crafting.

QUICK, EASY EMBELLISHING TECHNIQUES

Paper mosaics, layering, fabric collage, trimming, ribbon designs, thread effects, and enhancing images are some quick, easy techniques you can use. Below we'll describe how to do them.

Paper Mosaics

This easy technique mimics the look of broken-china mosaics in a fraction of the time and for a fraction of the cost, not to mention at a fraction of the weight. No more messy grout or waiting for your projects to dry. It also puts your endless paper scraps to good use. You can use wrapping paper, scrapbooking odds and ends, etc. If you don't have paper scraps on hand, magazine pages offer a wide array of intriguing colors and textures to play with. The papers can be randomly placed, as shown in the example given here (photo 1), or they can be more purposefully arranged to create designs and shapes.

✳ Apply a sheet of red-liner tape to the item you want to embellish. Peel back protective liner to expose sticky tape.

✳ Tear or cut bits of paper and adhere them directly onto the tape. You can apply them with your hands or bent-nose tweezers, as shown (photo 2). Vary the colors and textures of your paper scraps for best effect. For a different paper design, you can punch out mini paper shapes using cutter punches.

✳ Incorporate other embellishments into your paper designs. Anything goes, as long as it has a flat back to adhere firmly to the tape. Try buttons, threads, rhinestones, and ribbons, as well as all sorts of scrapbooking supplies. (See Layering on p. 20 for more about this.)

✳ When you are pleased with your design, place the decorated item in a shallow pan and pour clear glass microbeads or other small beads over the remaining exposed tape to fully cover (photo 3). For a different look, fill the exposed tape with glitter, colored sand, or other granular embellishments.

1 A finished paper mosaic.

2 Using tweezers to position paper scraps on tape.

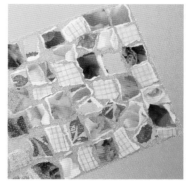

3 Swirl microbeads with fingertips to cover exposed tape.

Layering

Create a dramatic layered piece by starting with a paper mosaic and then adding another layer of embellishment on top. This increases the dimensional aspect of the design as well as its uniqueness. This technique is also useful when you are embellishing an awkwardly shaped surface and you want to make it look colorful, since tearing bits of paper and applying them to an irregularly shaped item is a lot easier than trying to apply a single sheet of paper or fabric to it.

❋ Once you have covered an item in papers, fabric, or glitter, you can add another layer of embellishment for more depth. Simply apply another layer of red-liner tape to the item, and peel back the protective liner to expose the sticky tape (photo 1).

❋ Create a design with all kinds of embellishments, from rhinestones to buttons to flat-back cabochons to decorative braid. The more varied the items you use, the more interesting the design (photo 2).

❋ When you are satisfied with your design, place the item in a shallow pan or tray and pour clear glass microbeads or other small beads over the remaining exposed tape to fully cover (photo 3).

1 Layering. Lifting the protective liner on the second sheet of tape.

2 Arranging beads over the tape sheet (right).

3 Adding microbeads (far right).

Fabric Collage

This fun technique uses fabric pieces with red-liner tape to create images like the American flag shown here. As with paper mosaics, this treatment is best achieved by using fabrics of a variety of colors and textures. The image you create can be done freestyle, or you can tape over an existing image and use it as a design template for embellishing. When using an image, you can cover the entire image with fabric bits, or, for a mixed-media effect, you can leave some of the original image showing through. Once you have completed your design, the exposed image areas can be covered with clear glass microbeads, giving the image underneath a 3-D effect.

Here are the steps to follow for a fabric collage:

❋ Apply a sheet of red-liner tape to the item you want to embellish. Next, peel back the protective liner to expose sticky tape.

❋ Cut fabric scraps into the desired shapes and adhere them directly onto tape by pressing them into place (photos 1 and 2).

❋ When you are satisfied with your design, place the collaged item in a shallow pan or tray and pour clear glass microbeads to cover the remaining exposed tape. Swirl with fingertips to fully cover all areas (photo 3).

❋ Tap the project on its side to dislodge loose beads. The finished flag is shown in photo 4.

1 Fabric collage. Starting to assemble the stripes on the tape layer.

2 Adding the blue scraps.

3 Adding microbeads to fill in the remaining space (far left).

4 The finished flag, filled with beads (left).

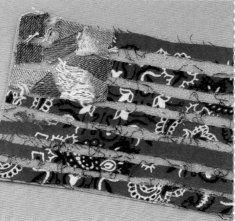

Trimming

This quick technique allows you to instantly apply all kinds of stringy stuff, like store-bought fabric trims, yarns, ribbons, and home decorating fringe, to your projects. Working with stringy stuff is particularly foolproof, since you can easily pull up your trim and start over if you are not pleased with it.

❊ Apply a strip of red-liner tape to whatever item you want to trim. Choose a width of red-liner tape based on the type of trimming you plan to do (photo 1). Then peel back the tape's protective liner to expose its sticky surface.

❊ Adhere the beaded fringe or other trim by pressing it directly onto the tape (photo 2). Use enough trim to cover the tape, plus about ¼". To start, fold the end of the trim under itself by about ⅛" and press it into the tape to create a no-sew seam. Continue applying trim to tape, almost to the tape's end. When you reach the end of the tape, tuck the other end of the trim under itself in the same manner as before and press it into the tape to finish. Terri O shows us an example on a fringed purse (photo 3).

1 Decorating a purse with trimming. Applying narrow red-liner tape across the top.

2 Pressing the fringe in place on the bag, over the tape (right).

3 A layer of fringe is now in place (far right). See Flapper-Girl Bag for more ideas.

Ribbon Designs

Here are some easy-to-do ribbon designs that we'll use in many projects.

Zigzagging

Apply ribbon to tape in a zigzag motion, pressing each zig and alternate zag directly onto the tape to secure it, as shown (photos 1 and 2).

"Smooshing"

Smooshing is my favorite ribbon application.

✳ Apply ribbon to a strip of red-liner tape that is wider than the ribbon you are using. For example, if the ribbon is ½" wide, use the ¾" tape.

✳ Start by pressing ¼" of the ribbon onto the tape in the opposite direction to the one in which you intend to go, in order to hide the cut end, prevent fraying, and create a no-sew seam (photo 3).

✳ Then literally smoosh (smash, jam, swirl) the ribbon this way and that in a random pattern. The tape will secure the ribbon wherever you press it into place (photo 4).

1 and **2** Zigzagging with ribbon.

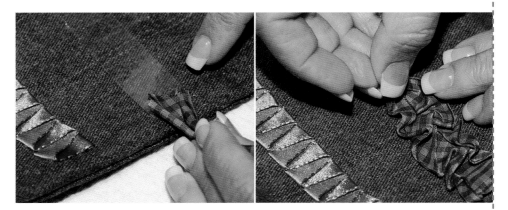

3 Adhering ribbon so end is turned under (far left).

4 "Smooshing" ribbon (left).

This may take a few practice tries, since it is more natural to try to place the ribbon in a controlled manner. Remember, with any stringy stuff, including ribbon, you can always pull it up and try again until you get it the way you like it.

Curling and Coiling

To apply curled ribbon or other decorations in this pattern, simply guide the ribbon downward, pressing it into the sticky tape, and then curve the ribbon upward again, as shown (photo 5). In this technique, the tape can be narrower than the ribbon curves you will create, as long as the curves are pressed securely to the tape along the center of the design, where the tape is. Try wired vs. unwired ribbon. You can also fold or roll up the ribbon as you apply it, for different effects.

5 Curling a wired trim down and up again.

Layering Ribbon

Layering allows you to create truly original designs. Start by applying ribbon in a straight line, as shown in photo 6. Then simply apply another strip of tape, narrower than the ribbon to which it is being applied to (photo 7), and add another ribbon design on top.

6 Layering ribbon. Applying ribbon to tape (right).

7 Applying more tape before adding a second layer of ribbon (far right).

Pleating

To pleat, loop ribbon with your finger, a craft stick, wooden skewer, or similar tool, and press the end of each loop onto the tape to secure the pleat. Continue to the end of the tape. This works beautifully with lace and with other flexible fabrics, too.

In the photo shown, the ribbon pleating is being layered on top of a straight line of ribbon in a complementary color; pleating can be done without layering, also.

8 Pleating ribbon, using a stick.

Looping Flower Petals

Looping works best with wired ribbon, which ensures that each loop really holds its shape. Curl the ribbon to create a loop and press the underside of the loop into the tape; repeat in a circular pattern to create a flower.

Ribbon Roses

Turn ribbons into roses in a jiffy simply by coiling them around a piece of tape. This is best accomplished with ¾"-wide wired ribbon, but other sizes will also work. With ¾" or wider ribbon, start by adhering a bit of tape to the surface you intend to decorate. Then fold the ribbon in half, and from the center of what will be the flower, coil the ribbon around itself, pressing the coils into the tape to secure them, while creating the rose shape. You can make any size you want. When you have completed your rose, snip off the ends of the ribbon and fold them under to hide the seam, pressing the folded ends onto the tape. These roses can be created on a strip of tape with more decorating done in between roses, or the roses can be created on precut tape circles.

9 Making flower petals from looped ribbon.

10 Ribbon roses made with wired ribbon.

To keep your ribbon or fringe from fraying, use clear nail polish at the end if you can't turn it under. —T. O.

Wrapping with Stringy Stuff

This is a great technique for adding flair to the handles of purses and bags, and for transforming ordinary headbands and pens into stylish statements. Almost any type of stringy stuff can be used. For example, you can wrap with knitting yarns, ribbons, old ties, decorative braids, and embroidery floss, as well as fringe and other trim.

❇ Apply a strip of tape (from a tape roll) lengthwise to one side of the item you want to wrap, such as the handbag handle shown here. Then simply peel back the protective liner to expose sticky tape (photo 11).

❇ Wrap the handle with ribbon by starting at the base of the handle and pressing the ribbon end onto the tape (photo 12). Wrap ribbon all the way around the handle, slightly overlapping each previous round as you go. Continue wrapping until the entire handle is covered. The decorated handle can be seen in photo 13.

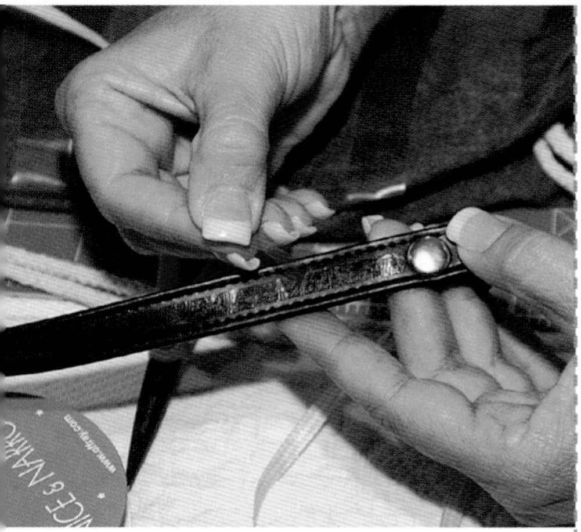

11 Applying the tape.

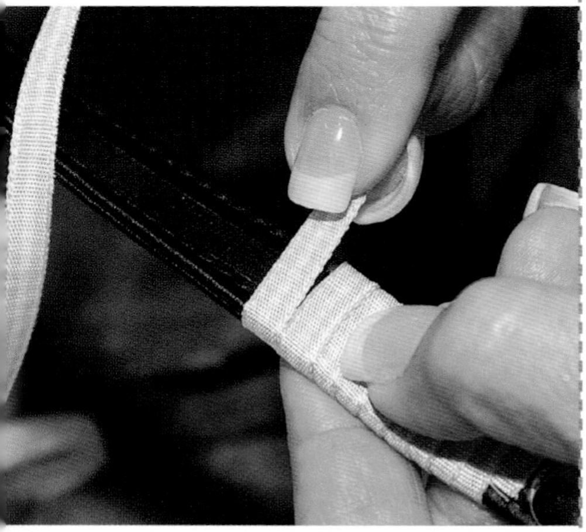

12 Wrapping the ribbon.

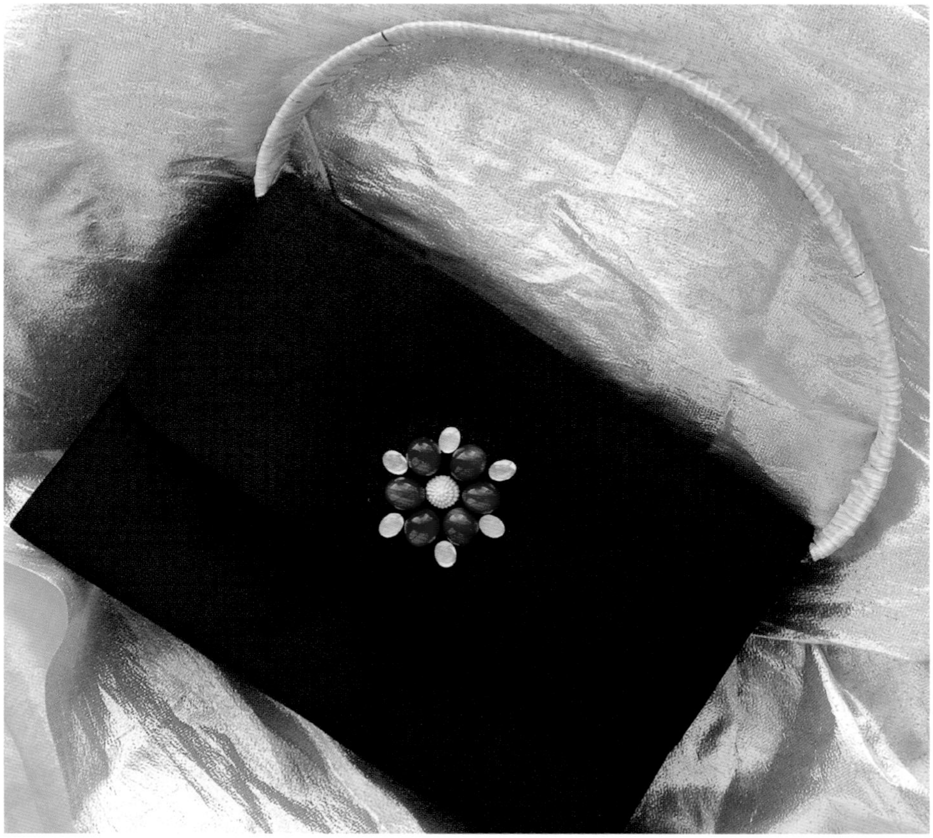

13 The finished handle.

Thread Designs

Create incredible faux embroidery designs instantly and easily by applying thin decorative braid or other decorative threads with red-liner tape. Decorative threads and braids come in a spectacular assortment of colors, textures, and sizes and look great with buttons, rhinestones, and other faux gems. Those of you who, like us, don't do any type of needlework now have a whole new world of embellishments to enjoy. Best of all, decorative braids and threads are quite forgiving, so once you lay them down, you can easily pull them back up and try again until you get it right.

❋ Apply red-liner tape to the item you want to embellish.

❋ Peel back the protective liner to expose the sticky tape (photo 1). Now you are ready to apply the decorative thread.

❋ Instantly "embroider" your project by "drawing" a decorative thread design directly onto the tape. This is done by guiding the braid or other thread with one hand while pressing it into place with the other (photo 2). If you prefer, an awl, craft stick, tweezers, or wooden skewer can be used to press the thread in place instead of your hand (photo 3). Once your thread design is complete, replace the top tape liner over the project and press all your threads firmly into the tape to fully secure them (photo 2).

❋ When you are pleased with your thread design, place the decorated item in a shallow pan and pour a granular embellishment such as clear glass microbeads over the remaining exposed tape to fully cover (photo 4).

1 Lifting the liner after the tape is in place.

2 Guiding the braid into place.

3 Pressing the braid to secure it (far left).

4 Adding clear glass microbeads (left).

Thread Writing

Another way to express yourself with decorative thread or braid is by writing words with it. Script writing is easiest, since you do not need to cut a separate thread for each letter.

✳ Prepare the words you will be outlining with threads. In photo 1, a rub-on copy of the word "love" was applied to scrapbook paper. (It also could have been written by hand on the paper.)

✳ Apply red-liner tape over the word or words to fully cover them (photo 2).

✳ Cut off a piece of decorative thread or braid that is the length you think you will need.

✳ Simply "write" with the thread or braid by guiding it with one hand and pressing it in place with your other hand or tweezers, as shown (photo 3).

✳ When you have finished writing with thread, pour clear glass microbeads (or glitter, etc.) over the remaining exposed tape to fully cover (photo 4) and swirl and press the beads in place.

1 Preparing the rub-on copy of the word.

2 Applying red-liner tape.

3 Writing with thread, using tweezers (right).

4 Applying microbeads (far right).

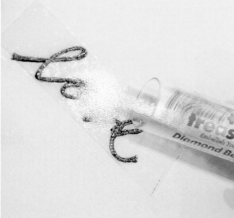

Image Transfer

Several projects in the book use photos, drawings, or other images as the starting off point for a creation. Fortunately, we're living in a time when transferring images onto paper or cloth is not hard to do. If you have a home computer, inkjet printer, and scanner, you can probably do this at home. If not, you can take your photo or other image to your local copy shop and have them scan and print it for you. In addition to being printed onto plain paper, images can be printed directly on fabric, or onto specially treated papers such as T-shirt transfer papers.

Printing Directly on Fabric: Printer Fabric Transfer Sheets

For printing directly on fabric, there are several brands of fabric transfer sheet on the market. These are pieces of stiffened cotton fabric bonded to paper, so that the sheet can be run through a home inkjet printer. Printing is done the same way as with copy paper. However, once the ink dries, you remove the paper backing, so that you can attach the transferred image to your project by sewing it, using an iron-on version of the fabric sheet, with red-liner tape, or some other way. Fabric transfer sheets typically can be found with quilting supplies as well as on the Internet.

Printing on Paper

Another method of using images is to print or copy them directly onto paper. This can be done by scanning them and printing them from your computer or by photocopying them on a color copy machine.

Printing on Transfer Paper

For stretchy items such as T-shirts, there are T-shirt transfers, specially treated papers that that create a decal-like transfer, which is then ironed onto a T-shirt or other clothing item. There are also other transfer papers that create water-slide decals (e.g., Lazertran Silk and Lazertran for Inkjet), which can then be placed on fabrics and other surfaces. Waterslide transfers need to dry before you do further work on them. Check out the requirements of each and use the one that is suited to your needs and computer setup. Visit your local copy shop for more information.

1 Bag with image photocopy.

2 Provence Handbag uses photo-copied pastel drawing as basis of design.

3 Brag Phone uses photocopy of pet photo.

1 Making a braid outline.

2 The decorated image.

Enhancing Images

Create an amazing 3-dimensional effect on your favorite images by applying crystal-clear glass microbeads over them. The images you use can come from almost anywhere. Before you bead the image, you can apply all sorts of other embellishments to really jazz it up. Once assembled, your homemade appliqué can be adhered to a variety of personal items, such as a canvas tote, backpack, notebook, or jeans jacket.

❋ Cover an image with a sheet of double-sided red-liner tape, trimmed to size, by peeling back one side of the tape's backing and then lining up the edges of the exposed tape with the edges of the image you intend to cover. Press the edges into place. Then slowly peel away the rest of backing from the tape sheet, pressing the tape sheet onto the image until the image is fully covered.

❋ Smooth out the tape by pressing it down with your fingertips, a credit card, or a brayer. If there are any air bubbles caught in the tape layer, you can try to push them to the edges and out; or use a craft knife or pin to pop them and then smooth out the affected area with your fingertips. Now, peel back the top protective liner to expose the sticky tape.

❋ Using the image under the tape as your design template, decorate it with all sorts of embellishments to create a unique work of art (photo 1). You can add a little bit of embellishment and let a lot of the image show through. At the other extreme, you can cover up the image completely.

❋ When you are pleased with your design, place the item in a shallow pan and pour clear glass microbeads over any remaining exposed tape. Swirl beads with fingertips to fully cover all tape areas and press beads in place. Tap the project on its side to dislodge any excess beads. The decorated image is shown in photo 2.

3 A decorated photo with a dog-theme border.

Projects & Ideas

WHAT'S YOUR BAG?

From elegant to whimsical, the purses and bags in this section offer you a range of ways of expressing yourself. Once you realize the power this gives you, you'll be able to create something that perfectly matches the mood and color of any outfit you have. No more running around to stores, looking for the perfect bag!

KEY

Time: up to 30 minutes

Techniques: trimming, layering, thread effects

Level of difficulty: beginner

MATERIALS

Faux-silk evening bag

Red-liner tape, ¼"-wide roll

Beaded-fringe trim

Thin decorative braid (12-strand braid)

Flapper-Girl Bag

designed by Terri O

Beaded trim makes sprucing up a plain evening bag a snap. You can add a single row of beaded trim, or, if you are feeling more decadent, add rows and rows to create a flapper-girl effect. Trims are also very easy to remove from your bag after use, so that your bag will be ready for a new look—unless of course you fall in love with your flapper-girl look and decide to keep it intact!

✳ Apply one row of red-liner tape across top of bag. Peel back red protective liner to expose sticky tape.

✳ Apply beaded-fringe trim to the exposed tape. Be sure to fold trim ends under and press firmly into tape to avoid fraying.

✳ Apply another strip of ¼"-wide red-liner tape over the ribbon part of the top row of the fringe and randomly curl and coil thin decorative braid over it to finish it off. You can stop here with one round or go on to create the flapper-girl bag.

✳ If desired, continue to adhere rows of beaded trim approximately ½" apart in the same way as the first row until the bag is fully embellished.

Note: Whenever you are using trim with many rows of things that dangle, always start from the bottom and work your way up, although this may seem counterintuitive. I initially started to make this bag from the top down and quickly realized that the beaded trim was in my way. Not to worry: I just pulled it off and saved it for later.

Rows of beaded-fringe clothing trim were added to a simple black bag with strips of red-liner tape.

Terri O Tips

• When you are out and about shopping, and you find a little black bag, buy it! You can create almost anything with it.

• You can add matching trim to your belt, shoes, and coat for a complete outfit, but don't go overboard. You will need to know when to stop!

Time: up to 30 minutes

Technique: trimming

Level of difficulty: beginner

MATERIALS

Handbag

Red-liner tape, ¼" wide

Small-tasseled home-decorating trim

Large-tassel trim for bottom of bag

Terri O Tips

• I love tassels. They are great for layering over each other or mixing with ribbon and beads.

• Don't forget that you can use the tape to add some tassels to your lampshades, too!

• I always say that it's the details that make a project stand out. When it comes to trim, that's detail.

Rows of fringe and tassels were added to this simple bag with strips of red-liner tape.

On-the-Fringe Bag

designed by Christina Santangelo

Tassel fringe, found in the home-decorating market and often spotted at tag sales and thrift shops, is great for turning an ordinary evening bag into a real conversation piece. Some of you may have odds and ends from past home-decorating projects tucked away, so it's time to dig them out. Tassels were too formal for my home, but I have always loved how handsome they look. Decorating a bag with them lets me enjoy their beauty in a more playful way.

Some of the many tassel fringes available.

❄ Apply a strip of ¼"-wide tape across the bag near the bottom, on both the front and back sides of the bag. Remember that tassels will hang down below the tape. Peel back the tape's protective liner to expose its stickiness.

❄ Adhere a row of small-tasseled trim by pressing it firmly into the tape. Don't forget to tuck each end of the trim under itself before pressing firmly into the tape, to create a no-sew seam and prevent fraying.

❄ You can cover the whole bag in the same fringe, adding more rows as shown here, or you can vary the types of fringe for a different effect.

❄ Add a strip of tape with larger, contrasting fringe at the very bottom of the bag to give it extra pizzazz.

Tag Sale Transformation

designed by Susan Zimmerman

There is nothing more satisfying than turning trash into a treasure, which is exactly what happened to the Cinderella bag on page 36. It was purchased for $1 at the end of a tag sale, having been passed over by most shoppers due to its dated, frumpy appearance. However, with a little imagination and a couple of embellishments from our cache of supplies, we gave it a second life, transforming it into a playful, colorful signature bag that gets attention everywhere it goes.

❄ Adhere a strip of ¼"-wide tape all around the top of the bag, about an inch or two down, as well as to the underside of the bag's handles. Also, apply ½" tape dots randomly to bag (for adhering flowers), but don't attach flowers yet.

❄ Peel back the top protective liner to expose the sticky tape as needed. Add the beaded fringe 1" or 2" down from the top of the bag, all the way around, pressing it onto the tape strip, tucking the ends under themselves.

❄ Wrap handles with trim or ribbon by starting at the base of the handle and wrapping around and around, overlapping slightly, until the handle is completely covered. Tuck trim ends under and press into tape to secure and to avoid fraying.

KEY

Time: up to 30 minutes

Techniques: wrapping, trimming, layering

Level of difficulty: beginner

MATERIALS

Tag-sale bag

Red-liner tape, ¼"-wide roll and ½" dots

Beaded fringe, about ½" wide

Trim or ribbon (for wrapping handles)

Silk flowers, pulled off their stem

Rhinestones

Glitter

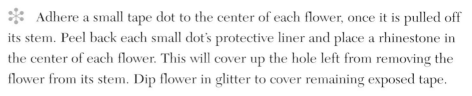

✻ Adhere a small tape dot to the center of each flower, once it is pulled off its stem. Peel back each small dot's protective liner and place a rhinestone in the center of each flower. This will cover up the hole left from removing the flower from its stem. Dip flower in glitter to cover remaining exposed tape.

✻ Apply each flower by adhering it to a tape dot on the bag.

The finished tag-sale bag sports silk flowers, trim, and beaded fringe.

They always say if you hold onto something long enough it comes back in style. Why wait? —T. O.

Ruffle Duffle

designed by Terri O

$\mathcal{R}$ibbon designs are so quick and satisfying to make that we went a little crazy on a couple of bags to showcase all the different ways to do it. Some of the effects, such as our signature "smooshing" technique, would be almost impossible to create on a sewing machine, making them even more exciting to do with tape. It took all of 20 minutes to decorate this cute denim tote. I smooshed, twisted, and turned the ribbon. Now it's a one-of-a-kind creation.

KEY

Time: 20 minutes

Techniques: ribbon designs, wrapping, trimming, layering

Level of difficulty: beginner

MATERIALS

Denim duffle

Red-liner tape, ¾"-wide roll

Assorted ribbons

Assorted buttons

Craft stick (ice cream bar stick)

Clear glass microbeads or glitter, colored sand, etc.

Buttons for denim duffle.

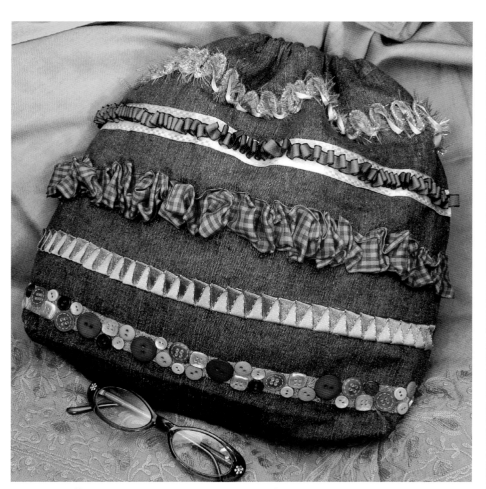

A denim duffle takes on personality when rows of decorative ribbon designs are added.

Here, a silk handbag is perked up for Easter by covering the flap and handle with assorted ribbon designs.

✳ Apply strips of ¾"-wide tape to bag as desired. You will peel back the top protective liner, one strip at a time, as you work.

✳ Create a ribbon design by guiding the ribbon with one hand and pressing it into place with the other. Use the craft stick for this if you wish. You can zigzag, curl, smoosh, pleat, layer, and wrap the ribbon onto the tape. (See Ribbon Designs on page 23 for step-by-step directions.)

✳ Add a row of assorted buttons along the bottom strip.

✳ If you haven't covered all areas of the tape in ribbon or other goodies, you will need to place the bag in a shallow container and pour clear glass microbeads (or glitter, colored sand, etc.) over any remaining exposed tape to fully cover it. Press the microbeads in place to adhere.

Terri O Tips

• To smoosh or not to smoosh? It's fun, it's easy, and it's a great way to frame, fill in, and finish off your design. So, when in doubt, smoosh!

• Play around with your ribbons. You might come up with a technique of your own. If you don't like the way they come out, just pull them off and start over.

An assortment of buttons.

Button Mania Bag

designed by Suzanne Chase

A simple evening bag takes on a whole new look when covered with an assortment of buttons and copper colored decorative braid. There are all sorts of places to find buttons, including spare buttons that come with clothing and buttons from clothing you no longer wear. The buttons shown here came from a shirt I bought because I liked the buttons. I barely wore it, because it wasn't flattering on me. Now I can finally wear the buttons on something that suits me!

❋ Cover the flap of the bag with red-liner tape by trimming an 8" x 10" sheet to size and adhering it to the flap. To do this, peel off the tape's backing and press the tape firmly into place. If you are using scraps instead of a trimmed sheet, you can overlap tape if necessary by adhering one piece and then peeling back its top liner and adhering the next piece. When the flap is fully covered, peel back any remaining protective liner to expose sticky tape.

❋ Create a border around the flap by adhering buttons around the perimeter. Then randomly adhere assorted buttons to the rest of the flap, leaving spaces between buttons in which to swirl the decorative braid. Swirl decorative braid (a somewhat thick, 32-strand braid was used) between the buttons by guiding the braid with one hand and pressing it into place with an awl, craft stick, or tweezers with the other. Replace the tape's top liner over embellished flap and press all braid into place to make sure it is secure.

❋ Place the handbag in a shallow pan and pour black sparkling sand over remaining exposed tape. Swirl sand with fingertips to fully cover tape. Tap bag on its side to dislodge loose sand.

KEY

Time: up to 1 hour

Techniques: basic embellishing, thread effects

Level of difficulty: intermediate

MATERIALS

Satin-finish evening bag with flap

Red-liner tape, 8" x 10" sheet

Assorted buttons

Decorative copper-colored metallic braid (32-strand braid)

Black sparkling sand

Awl, craft stick, or tweezers

Evening bag with decorative buttons and metallic copper braid swirled in between for added texture.

Terri O Tips

• If you need to, you can bend the charms to fit the curve of your handbag. You can also bend things (e.g., the petals on flowers) for added dimension. Please note, however, embellishments will be most secure if they are flush against the tape.

• Think layers. Metal over ribbon or beads over metal can give your project a whole new look.

Terri O to Go Bag

designed by Terri O

*M*ake a statement with your bag by writing your name on it in handsome metal letter charms. In addition to your name, you can communicate all kinds of other things too, such as an attitude, belief, or sentiment, and then strut it around town. There are many fun little trinkets out on the market today, thanks to scrapbooking. Do what I do: wander the aisles and let your imagination go! I made a bag like this as a gift for someone. She was very excited to know that I took the time to make something just for her.

Metal scrapbooking charms were used to embellish this little bag. Decorative metallic thread adds extra shimmer.

Trim the tape sheet to fit area of bag you intend to decorate. Peel backing off tape sheet and adhere to bag. Peel off the tape's top protective liner to expose stickiness.

Adhere metal letter charms to bag by pressing gently into tape. Next, curl, coil, and swirl decorative threads all around lettering and remaining exposed tape areas. Do this by guiding the threads with one hand while pressing them into place with the other. Here, Japan thread that has the look of strung liquid silver beads was used.

When you have completed your design, place the bag in a shallow pan and pour clear glass microbeads (or glitter) over the remaining exposed tape. Swirl beads with fingertips to fully cover the tape, and then tap project on its side to dislodge any loose beads.

Finish off the bag by tying a decorative bow to the handle.

Metal charms.

Tapestry Evening Bag

designed by Suzanne Chase

The handbag on page 42 was transformed into a textural work of art with fabric swatches that I had on hand after couch-shopping. I kept the tapestry style swatches (albeit buried in the bottom of a bag in my hall closet) because I liked them. Now, with a bit of ribbon and embroidery thread, I can show them off on a sophisticated bag that mimics a crazy-quilt design.

Cover the flap of the bag with red-liner tape by trimming an 8" x 10" sheet to size, peeling the backing off the tape, and pressing tape firmly onto the flap. If you are using scraps of tape instead of a trimmed sheet, you can overlap tape when necessary by adhering one piece, and then peeling back its top liner and adhering the next piece. When the flap is fully covered, peel back any remaining protective liner to expose the sticky tape.

Cut fabric swatches into different-shaped pieces to mimic the look of a crazy quilt. Adhere pieces of fabric close to one another by pressing into place on the tape.

KEY

Time: 1 hour

Techniques: fabric collage, thread effects, layering

Level of difficulty: intermediate

MATERIALS

Faux-silk evening bag with flap

Red-liner tape, 8" x 10" sheet and ¼" wide roll

Tapestry fabric swatches

Decorative threads and braid for outlining

Large decorative button or embellishment

½"-wide ribbon for outlining flap and wrapping handle

Fabric swatches of couch material.

✳ When flap is fully covered in fabric, apply ¼"-wide strips of tape along the edges of adjacent pieces of fabric to create faux stitch seams between them. Peel back the top protective liner on the strips. Zigzag assorted decorative threads onto the taped seams to imitate crazy quilt stitches.

✳ Place bag in a shallow pan and pour clear glass microbeads over any remaining exposed tape. Swirl with fingertips to fully cover. Tap bag on its side to dislodge loose beads.

✳ Apply ¼"-wide tape around perimeter of bag's flap and peel back the top liner to expose sticky tape.

✳ Smoosh ribbon onto the exposed tape to create a fanciful ribbon frame around the crazy-quilt design. Wrap the handle in ribbon also, after covering the inside of it with ¼"-wide red-liner tape.

✳ Apply a decorative button or embellishment to the center of the flap with tape scraps.

Terri O Tips

• Here is the great thing about fabric swatches: if you really like a certain pattern, you can have it in several colors!

• Many upholstery shops throw out their swatches on a regular basis since styles change so quickly, so why not make a bag for the store manager; then you'll get all the swatches you'll ever need, for free!

Zigzagged decorative threads were taped around each piece of upholstery fabric to create a hand-sewn effect.

Fiber-Crazy Knitting Bag

designed by Suzanne Chase

We hope this project will inspire knitters and needleworkers to make their needlework totes as artistic and beautiful as the projects that the bags hold. This bag's motif is made from all sorts of yarn, buttons, ribbon, and fabric odds and ends that you might have on hand if you are into sewing or other needle crafts, so it was easy and inexpensive to decorate.

KEY

Time: 1 hour, plus

Techniques: image embellishing, ribbon designs, thread effects

Level of difficulty: advanced

MATERIALS

Canvas or denim tote or needlework bag

Red-liner tape, 8" x 10" sheet and 1"-wide strips

Piece of decorative fabric, sized to fit the front of the bag

Assorted buttons, ribbons, yarns, sequins, ricrac, and fibers

Clear glass microbeads, glitter, or other granular embellishment

A piece of colorful fabric was used as the design template for creating this playful bag. All kinds of fibers were used to recreate the fabric design.

There is something about this bag I love! It speaks to me. It screams "creativity!" —T. O.

The fabric that inspired the Fiber-Crazy Knitting Bag.

Terri O Tips

• If you are not a knitter or into sewing and you want a variety of fibers and ribbons to work with, look in scrapbooking stores for their color-coordinated assortments of fibers.

• You can do a lot of embellishing and have none of the decorative fabric show through or do some embellishing and allow the fabric image to show through.

✳ Tack the decorative fabric, well centered, onto the front of the tote with tape scraps, a tape sheet, or strips of red-liner tape. Then adhere a sheet of tape, trimmed to size, over the decorative fabric. Do not worry if the tape sheet is larger than the fabric. To adhere, peel back two corners of the tape sheet, match them up to the corresponding two corners of the fabric, and press into place. Continue to peel the backing off the tape sheet while pressing the tape into place as you go. When covering fabric, you will be able to pull up the tape sheet and reposition it if necessary.

✳ Once the fabric is adhered, smooth the tape out over the fabric with your hand, a brayer, a credit card, etc. If there are any air bubbles, simply prick them with a pin or other sharp object and then smooth out the tape.

✳ Once tape is smoothed out, peel back its top protective liner to expose stickiness.

✳ Using the decorative fabric's pattern as a design template, start embellishing it by adhering yarns, ribbons, buttons, and fibers directly onto the tape. You can curl, coil, smoosh, or zigzag your ribbons. See Ribbon Designs and Thread Effects on pages 23 and 27 for detailed instructions and ideas.

✳ Apply strips of 1"-wide tape around the borders of the decorative fabric and embellish with additional ribbon and/or button designs.

✳ When you are pleased with your design, place the bag in a shallow container and pour clear glass microbeads (or glitter, sand, etc.) over any remaining exposed tape areas. Swirl with fingertips to fully cover. Tap bag on its side to dislodge excess beads.

Provence Handbag

designed by Suzanne Chase

Using your own artwork (or that of a close friend or family member) as the design template for embellishing an evening bag offers a profoundly personal craft opportunity and gorgeous results. Here, I took a digital photo of a pastel that I had created a few years ago in an art class and printed it from my computer to fit the face of this plain black evening bag. For me, an added value about this motif is that not only did I create the drawing, but the image drawn in pastel was from a photo of a sentimental trip I had taken with my husband.

KEY

Time: 2 hours

Techniques: image embellishing, trimming, thread designs, ribbon designs

Level of difficulty: advanced

MATERIALS

Plain black handbag

Artwork image

Printer fabric sheets for image transfer

Red-liner tape, 8" x 10" sheet, plus scraps

Assorted beads, colors to match artwork

Decorative braids and dimensional embroidery threads, colors to match artwork

Clear glass microbeads

Assorted trims and ribbons (here, vintage trims were used)

This handbag showcases an image that was originally a pastel drawing.

• Use this technique to create gorgeous decorative pillows, to make wall hangings (the image can be adhered to a velvet panel and hung on a dowel), or to cover a simple leather jewelry box found in a discount store.

• Printer fabric sheets work with color copiers to make colorfast transfers directly onto fabric. This is great for wearable projects.

❋ Copy artwork onto a printer fabric sheet that is designed for image transfer (see page 29), sized to fit the item you intend to decorate. For pastel drawings or items larger than your scanner, you could take a digital photo of the piece and then print it from your computer onto the fabric sheet.

❋ Remove the paper backing from the image on fabric. Tack the artwork on fabric onto the front of the handbag with tape scraps, a tape sheet, or strips of tape. Then apply a sheet of red-liner tape, trimmed 1" larger than artwork on all sides, over it. To adhere the tape sheet, peel back two corners of the tape sheet liner, align them 1" above the corresponding corners of the image on fabric, and press into place. Continue to peel the backing off the tape sheet while pressing the tape into place.

❋ Smooth tape out with your hand or with a brayer. If there is an air bubble, you can prick it with a pin or other sharp object and then smooth out the tape. Peel back the top protective liner to expose tape.

❋ Using the art image as your guide, embellish it with assorted decorative braids, threads, and beads. Apply threads by guiding them with one hand while pressing them into place with the other. The beads can be applied to the tape by sprinkling them with your hands or placing them more precisely with

Before beading. Closeup of the photocopied pastel image with beads.

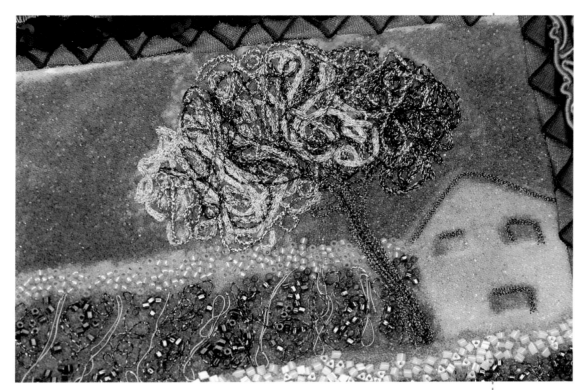

Closeup of the beaded and decorated image.

Doesn't this bag belong in a museum? Notice how Suzanne used different colors and shapes of glass beads to add color and texture. This proves that a work of art can do more than just hang on the wall. Wow! —T. O.

tweezers. The more varied the colors and textures, the better the result. You can choose to cover most of the image with threads and beads, or just highlight areas and leave parts of the image showing through for a mixed-media effect.

✱ Frame the image with ribbon designs or decorative trim by applying them to the 1" sticky border that was created when you trimmed your tape 1" larger than the artwork on all sides. In the project shown, purple ribbon was zig-zagged around the entire border first, and then vintage trims were added. Additional strips of tape were added so that trims covered the entire front of the bag.

✱ Once you are finished embellishing, place the bag in a shallow container and pour clear glass microbeads over remaining exposed tape. Swirl with fingertips to fully cover.

Foil flecks used on clutch.

A Brilliant Clutch

designed by Suzanne Chase

*S*tun your friends with this brilliant bag made entirely out of tape! The bag is made from a sheet of red-liner tape adorned with vintage trim, embroidery threads, cabochons, and gold foil flecks on one side, and a scrapbooking fabric sheet on the other. To hold the bag together, a no-sew seam was created with ¼"-wide red-liner tape. Perfect for festive evenings when all you need is some lipstick, tissues, and a cell phone.

❋ Peel off the backing of the red-liner tape sheet and adhere it to a 7" x 10" piece of fabric. Trim taped fabric to 6" x 9". Place sheet on table, fabric side up. To create the clutch shape without sewing, apply a strip of ¼"-wide tape along the left and right edge of the fabric, starting 1½" down from the top and continuing to the bottom. Peel back the tape's top protective liner to expose sticky tape. Fold the taped part of the fabric sheet onto itself, so that the strips of exposed tape are folded in half and are pressed together to create the clutch shape with a no-sew seam. Please note, you should end up with 1½" of fabric left unfolded at the top. This will be folded over later as a flap for the clutch. If this arrangement did not happen, peel off the ¼" tape from edges and reapply 1½" down from top to leave room for the flap.

❋ To embellish with assorted trims, remove the liner from the tape sheet on the front of the clutch, and apply trims to the tape, creating rows of texture, pattern, and color. When the entire front side of the clutch is covered in trim, apply a new strip of ¼" tape down both sides of clutch, covering over the trim ends. Then adhere decorative trim along sides. Don't forget to tuck trim ends under and press them into the tape to avoid fraying.

❋ When finished, flip clutch over to other side and remove the tape liner on the back of the clutch. Embellish the back with gold flecks and ultra-fine glitter. This is done by sprinkling gold foil flecks randomly over exposed red-liner

I must say, this is one of my favorites! Bead a strap for the shoulder, and let your friends be jealous. —T. O.

tape and then pressing the flecks into place. A little goes a long way. Once flecks are secured, sprinkle ultra-fine glitter over remaining exposed tape areas to fully cover.

✳ Next, layer circular tape shapes in various sizes on top of the embellished tape. Peel back top liners and adhere buttons or cabochons to the centers of the circles to be flower centers. "Embroider" around the buttons with metallic embroidery thread by guiding the thread with one hand and pressing it into place with the other.

✳ Add a decorative button to the center of the flap with tape scraps.

✳ To round the corners of the flap, cut freehand with scissors (or make an outline on cardboard to follow).

✳ When embellishing the circular tape shapes is done, place clutch over a paper plate and spoon ultra-fine glitter over any remaining exposed tape to fully cover it.

Terri O Tips

• No matter what you do with it, glitter is messy. Be sure you tap off all the excess as best you can. You don't want it on your party dress.

• Foil gives any project you do a beautiful finish. If you have never worked with it before, I suggest you practice on something else first.

• Foil comes in flakes or in 4" x 4" sheets. For spot-foiling, flakes work great, while sheets are best for larger projects.

Front of clutch.

Back of clutch.

A BRILLIANT CLUTCH   49

WHAT'S IN YOUR BAG?

You carry these items with you every day, so why settle for boring designs and dull colors? Put your own personal stamp on these familiar items, from compact to cell phone.

KEY

Time: up to 15 minutes per item

Techniques: wrapping, layering, thread designs

Level of difficulty: beginner

MATERIALS

Makeup compacts, lipsticks, makeup brushes, etc., to decorate

Red-liner tape, 1"- and ¼"-wide rolls, ½" and ¼" dots

Textured papers or fabrics

Assorted small buttons

Assorted small iridescent cabochons and small, round mosaic tiles

Ultra-fine glitter

Ribbon for brush, wide and narrow

Decorative threads

Makeup Madness

designed by Suzanne Chase & Susan Zimmerman

Just when we thought we had covered everything, we started decorating our makeup compacts. So now we can touch up our makeup in public and, instead of being ridiculed, become the envy of all those around us. Be warned: Once you give this idea a whirl, you may have trouble stopping. Bejeweled makeup compacts and lipsticks make great gifts, and they can provide a novel activity for a get-together with your girlfriends.

Makeup items were jazzed up with all sorts of goodies, applied with red-liner tape.

Bejeweled Lipstick Case

❋ Cover the lipstick case in tape by adhering strips around the cover and the base. You can overlap the strips if necessary by pulling the top liner off a strip already laid down before layering another strip over it. Apply tape dots to the top and bottom of the lipstick. When lipstick case is covered in tape, remove protective liner from tape to expose its sticky surface.

❋ Adhere different-sized cabochons and small, round mosaic tiles to the lipstick case by pressing them gently into the tape. You can apply them randomly (as shown here) or in a pattern. Adhere a decorative button or a cabochon to the top and bottom of the lipstick.

❋ When you are pleased with your design, hold the lipstick case over a shallow pan and spoon ultra-fine glitter over to cover any remaining exposed tape.

Plain and decorated lipstick cases.

Button Compact

❋ Apply strips of tape (or tape sheet, trimmed to size) to the top of the compact. Peel back top protective liner.

A trio of lipstick cases sport embroidery thread, metal mesh, and rhinestones.

❋ Adhere a textured paper or fabric, trimmed to size, to the compact cover by lining up edges of paper with corresponding edges of tape and pressing gently. Adhere assorted buttons with red-liner tape dots or tape scraps.

I must admit I thought my new gal pals were crazy, but once again they proved me wrong. When I pull out my compact, my friends say, "Make one for me!" —T. O.

Spiraled Blush Brush

✻ Adhere ¼"-wide tape lengthwise down one side of the brush. Peel back tape's protective liner.

✻ Cover entire brush handle in ribbon by wrapping the ribbon around and around, overlapping slightly, until brush handle is fully covered. Don't forget to tuck ribbon ends under and press them firmly into the tape to prevent fraying.

✻ Spiral another strip of ¼" tape around the brush handle. Peel back top liner. Attach a narrow ribbon over the spiraled tape.

✻ Adhere faux jewels around spiraled ribbon with small tape dots.

✻ Hold item over a shallow pan and spoon glitter onto any remaining exposed tape. Tap brush on its side to dislodge excess glitter.

Eye-Shadow Compact

✻ Trace the lid and cut out and adhere a circle of red-liner tape to the lid; then use small mosaic tiles to create the design. Next, place decorative threads around tiles to complete the design.

✻ Hold item over a shallow pan and spoon glitter onto any remaining exposed tape. Tap the compact on its side to dislodge excess glitter.

We had no problem finding stuff to embellish. For starters, just empty out your purse and see what you find. While you're at it, take the time to clean it out! —T. O.

Eye-shadow compact.

Perky To-Do Book

designed by Terri O

If you rely on a memo book throughout the day, why not make it spectacular looking? This adorable pooch is a fabric design that was adhered to the cover of a memo book and brought to life with fancy metallic threads. Fabrics are a great source of images for embellishing, as they come in all different styles and sizes to match your whim. For extra pizzazz, chenille yarn (left over from knitting a sweater) frames the image, giving the book a rich, soft texture.

KEY

Time: less than 1 hour

Technique: image embellishing

Level of difficulty: intermediate

MATERIALS

Small spiral notebook

Red-liner tape, 8" x 10" sheet

Fabric image

Chenille yarn

Round glass mosaic tiles

Decorative metallic threads (32-strand and 12-strand braids)

Clear glass microbeads (use clear ones so the image will show through)

A fabric with an adorable doggy print was the starting point.

Fabric for the notebook cover.

✳ Trim your fabric slightly smaller than the cover of the notebook. (Here, the fabric was approximately ½" smaller on three sides and 1" smaller on the bottom.)

✳ Tack fabric to notebook cover with red-liner tape scraps or strips of tape. Trim a sheet of tape to fit over entire notebook cover, and adhere by peeling down the top of the paper backing on the tape sheet and lining the edges up with the corresponding edges of the notebook cover. Gently press tape edges into place. Then slowly peel the remaining backing off the tape sheet while pressing the tape onto the cover as you go.

✳ Smooth out tape on cover with your hand, a brayer, etc. Peel back the top protective liner to expose sticky tape.

✳ Using the fabric design as your guide, draw over images with decorative threads by guiding them with one hand and pressing them into place with the other. Here, the dog was decorated with metallic embroidery threads. For added effect, the threads were frayed on the ends to make the dog's tail fluffy. Small round mosaic tiles were placed over the fabric's dot design, and then additional threads were swirled in between.

✳ We used a gorgeous chenille yarn to frame the embellished fabric image. This was done by curling the yarn back and forth over the remaining exposed tape. Each end of the yarn was pressed firmly into the tape to secure.

✳ When your design work is complete, place the notebook in a shallow pan and pour clear glass microbeads over to fully cover any remaining exposed tape. Tap notebook on its side to dislodge loose beads. Because the beads are clear, they will allow the image underneath to show through while providing a 3-D effect.

Terri O Tips

• It's all in the fabric with this project. The outline was already there; all I had to do was follow it. How easy is that?

• Before you begin, try laying everything out to see if you like it. That way, when you are ready to sit down to work, you can finish your project quickly and move on to the next one.

Mah Jong Address Book

designed by Suzanne Chase

Address books provide another great surface on which to express yourself. Here, a note card picture of mah jong tiles was used to show off a favorite hobby. Another option, with deeper personal meaning, is to use the image from a special note you received from a loved one. That way, you'll have a daily reminder of its invaluable sentiment.

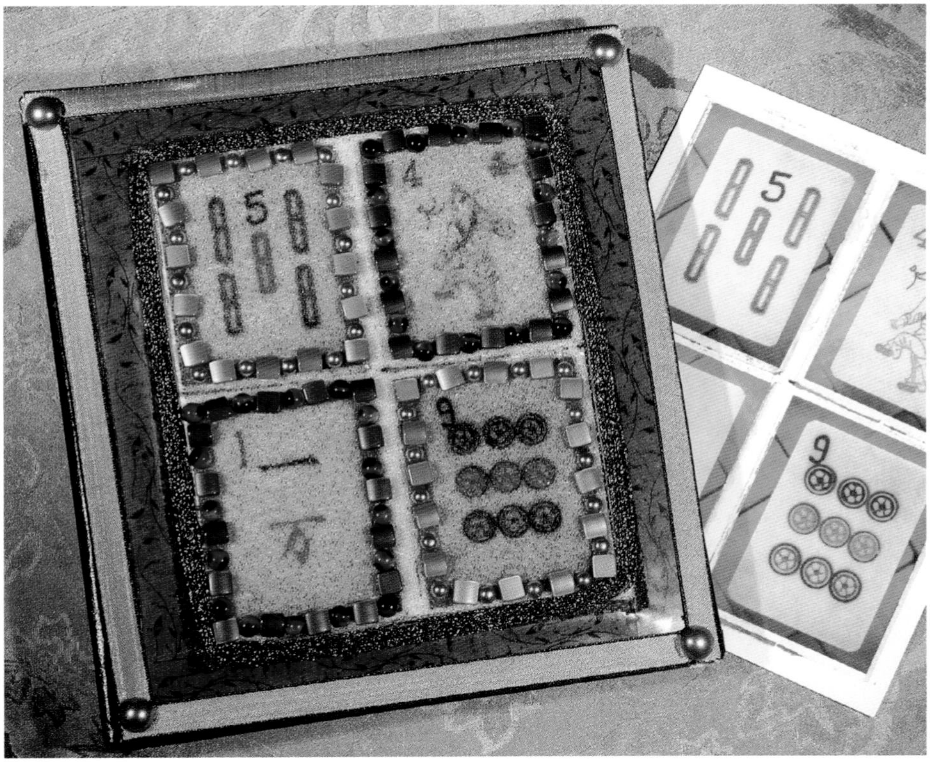

The address book cover began with a favorite note card image of mah jong tiles.

Tack front of card onto center of address book with scraps or strips of tape. Next, trim tape sheet to size of notebook cover. Peel backing off top edges of the tape, line the edges up with the corresponding edges of the notebook cover, and press into place. Continue to peel the remaining backing off tape sheet while pressing onto notebook cover. When backing is all the way off, smooth tape out over image with hand or brayer.

KEY

Time: 45 minutes

Techniques: image embellishing, trimming, thread effects

Level of difficulty: intermediate

MATERIALS

Address book

Red-liner tape, 8" x 10" sheet, plus scraps

Note card image or other image

Decorative metallic braid (green)

Lucite mosaic tiles and cabochons

Faux-pearl cabochons

Ribbon, ¼" wide

Scrapbook sticker borders

Clear glass microbeads

Supplies for book cover include ribbon and metallic thread.

❋ Using the card image as a design template, embellish the image to your liking. Here, small Lucite cabochons and mosaic tiles were used to frame the mah jong tiles.

❋ Decorative metallic braid was used to frame the card. Next, scrapbooking sticker borders were applied as an additional frame to the image. Finally, ¼" ribbon was applied in strips to the outer edges of the notebook cover. To hide the ribbon ends, faux-pearl cabochons were adhered to each corner with scrap tape.

❋ Once design work is complete, place the item in a shallow container and pour clear glass microbeads over remaining exposed tape to fully cover any remaining sticky areas, while allowing the card image to show through. What a fun way to be a part of the mah jong rage!

Terri O Tips

• To hide ribbon ends, cover them up with a button, mosaic tile, or a jewelry cabochon.

• If your book cover design ends up a little off center, just use ribbon to even out the design. No one will ever know!

• For the holidays, I decorated the covers of several address books to give as gifts. I made a few extra for those last-minute gift bags. Everybody needs one, and they're inexpensive to buy and embellish.

ON THE PHONE

Flaunt your personal style (or photos of your loved ones) by adorning your cell phone with all sorts of goodies. Photographs, rhinestones, scrapbook papers, and metallic embroidery threads all make perfect embellishments. Embellishing your phone not only makes a statement, it also helps differentiate you and your phone from the rest of the pack.

A group of embellished cell phones take on personality when decorated with scrapbooking supplies, origami papers, mosaic tiles, fabric, ribbon, rhinestones, and buttons.

Time: 30 minutes

Techniques: layering, thread designs

Level of difficulty: beginner

MATERIALS

Cell phone

Red-liner tape, 4" x 6" sheet and ⅛"-wide roll

Origami paper

Scrapbooking border stickers

Mosaic tiles

Decorative metallic embroidery thread (12-strand)

Supplies for Origami Phone.

Origami Phone

designed by Suzanne Chase

*M*osaic tiles are a great source of embellishment for red-liner tape craft-ing. Here, colorful tiles are paired with beautiful origami papers to create a colorful Eastern motif on this cell phone.

Origami Cell Phone.

❈ Trim a sheet of red-liner tape to fit over the back of your cell phone and adhere it by peeling off backing and pressing into place.

❈ Trim origami paper to fit over the back of your cell phone and apply to tape by adhering the top two corners to tape first and then pressing the remainder of paper onto the tape, gradually peeling down the tape liner. Next, apply scrapbooking border stickers around edges of phone to frame it.

❈ Frame the inside and outside edges of the scrapbook border with strips of ⅛"-wide tape. Peel back top protective liners.

❈ Decorate with metallic embroidery thread (12-strand was used here) by pressing the thread directly into the tape.

❈ Apply mosaic tiles to center of phone back with tape scraps.

Terri O Tips

• If edges are uneven or don't look finished, simply add strips of tape around phone to frame, and create another layer of embellishing. Framing seems to finish off just about any project you may do.

• Make sure your design doesn't get in the way of closing your phone properly or being able to charge it.

Here, a metal fiber sheet and shell buttons are used to embellish another phone in a similar manner to the Origami Phone, but yielding a very different look.

Time: 30 minutes

Techniques: image embellishing, thread designs

Level of difficulty: advanced beginner

MATERIALS

Cell phone

Red-liner tape, 4" x 6" sheet

Fabric swatch (or note card, etc.) with image of cat

Rhinestones

Decorative embroidery threads (12-strand)

Ribbon, ¼"

Clear glass microbeads

Masking tape

Supplies and (right) Cat Chat Phone.

Cat Chat Phone

designed by Suzanne Chase

This phone is purr-fect for cat lovers and those who enjoy French flair. An adorable fabric print was used as the design template for decorating with embroidery threads, rhinestones, and ribbon. You can find fabrics in sewing and quilting stores; they also are sold as stiffened and cropped 12" x 12" squares for scrapbooking.

Note: As with any electronic device, you should protect the openings of your cell phone with masking tape before you bead it. If any beads get inside, they may ruin your phone or block the adapter opening.

✳️ Trim a sheet of tape to fit over the back of your cell phone and adhere it by peeling its backing off and pressing it into place.

✳️ Trim fabric swatch and apply it to the tape by lining up the top edges with the tape's corresponding edges and pressing into place, gradually peeling down the tape's top liner.

✳️ Apply another layer of tape, trimmed to size, over the fabric swatch, and then peel back the tape's protective liner to expose the stickiness.

✳️ Outline the fabric design with decorative embroidery threads (12-strand was used here) by applying them directly onto the tape. To do this, guide the thread with one hand while pressing it into place with the other. You can also use an awl, tweezers, or a craft stick to press the threads into place, if you prefer.

✳️ For extra flair, you can embellish the fabric image with other goodies, such as the rhinestones used here, by sticking them directly onto the tape.

✳️ Protect phone openings with masking tape. Place project in a shallow pan and pour clear glass microbeads over the remaining exposed tape. Swirl beads with fingertips to fully cover tape. Tap project on its side to dislodge loose beads.

Terri O Tips

• If, when applying red-liner tape to any project, you find it is a little short, no worries. Just peel off the top liner of the already-applied tape, and add on another piece where you need it. The tape is thin like plastic wrap, so the overlap area will not show, especially when embellishing is done over it.

Scrapbooking paper was the basis of this design.

MATERIALS

Cell phone

Red-liner tape, 4" x 6" sheet

Clear glass microbeads

Favorite photo of pet

Bandana

Scrapbooking paper

Masking tape

Supplies for Brag Phone.

Brag Phone

designed by Susan Zimmerman

For some of us, it's torture leaving the little guy at home, so here is a way to bring your favorite pet wherever you go, regardless of the "No Pets Allowed" signs that abound. Bits of an old bandana are perfect for dressing up your new pet phone.

❋ Get a color photocopy of the photo you wish to use.

❋ Apply red-liner tape to back of cell phone. You can use strips of tape or a tape sheet trimmed to size. Once you have applied the tape to the phone, peel back the tape's protective liner to expose its stickiness.

❋ Trim the photocopy and position it on the phone back.

❋ Snip bits of the bandana and adhere them to some areas of the phone by gently pressing them into the exposed tape. You can add bits of scrapbooking paper or other fabric, too, for variation. (Here, cream-colored paper was used.)

❋ Protect the openings in the phone with masking tape, place the phone in a shallow pan, and pour clear glass microbeads over remaining exposed red-liner tape. Swirl beads with fingertips to fully cover. Tap phone on its side to dislodge excess beads.

Brag Phone.

English Garden Phone

designed by Suzanne Chase

For a more sophisticated look, a swatch of paper fashioned after a popular vintage wallpaper design is paired with an English country die-cut flower. The die-cut has an embroidered look, and the bow adds a flirtatious grace to an otherwise dull cell phone (photo on p. 64).

❄ Apply tape to cell phone back. You can use strips of tape or a tape sheet trimmed to size. Once you have applied the tape to the phone, peel back the tape's top protective liner to expose its stickiness.

❄ Cut the swatch of wallpaper to fit over the back of the cell phone, and adhere it to the sticky tape by lining up the corners of the paper with the corners of the tape and pressing them gently into place. Continue pressing the remainder of the paper onto the tape and then smooth it out.

KEY

Time: 30 minutes

Techniques: enhancing images, thread designs

Level of difficulty: advanced beginner

MATERIALS

Cell phone

Red-liner tape, sheet or ¼" and ⅛" rolls

Swatch of wallpaper or other pretty paper

Die-cut flower or other flower image

Bows

Dimensional embroidery threads

Clear glass microbeads

Terri O Tips

- Using the end of your tweezers or an awl, press the threads into the tape to make sure they are secure before you pour on the beads.
- Don't forget to decorate your phone case to match!

English Garden Phone.

❋ Trim a piece of tape the shape of the die-cut flower. Next, adhere the trimmed tape sheet over the die-cut. Peel off the top protective liner to expose the tape's stickiness.

❋ "Embroider" the die-cut flower with dimensional embroidery thread, using the image underneath as your design template. Do this by guiding the threads with one hand while pressing them into place with the other.

✳ Dip the "embroidered" die-cut in clear microbeads to fill in any remaining exposed tape, and adhere the die-cut to the center of the cell phone back with scraps of tape.

✳ Apply strips of ¼" tape to the top and bottom of the phone, above and below the paper that is already adhered on the back, and apply ⅛" tape along the sides. Decorate the strips of tape with threads in coordinating colors.

✳ Apply a strip of ¼" tape lengthwise to the underside of the phone's antenna. Peel off the tape's top liner. Decorate the antenna by wrapping additional embroidery thread around it.

✳ When design is complete, place phone in a shallow pan and pour clear glass microbeads over if there is any remaining exposed tape. Swirl with fingertips to fully cover. Tap phone on its side to dislodge excess beads.

Supplies for English Garden Phone.

Country French Phone

designed by Suzanne Chase

Torn bits of scrap paper in country French colors give the cell phone on page 66 the look of a broken-china mosaic without all the weight and sharp edges of real broken china. Looping wired ribbon into a flower creates a festive center appliqué. The ribbon used is called ombre (which means "shadow" in French), recognized by its hand-dyed, multicolored look.

✳ Apply red-liner tape to cell phone back. You can use strips of tape or a tape sheet trimmed to size. Once you have applied the tape to the phone, peel back its protective top liner to expose stickiness.

✳ Apply dimensional embroidery thread around the perimeter of the cell phone to frame it, guiding the thread with one hand and pressing it into place with the other. Trim thread end and press firmly into the tape to avoid fraying.

✳ Next, tear bits of decorative papers and adhere them to the taped phone by gently pressing them into place. Vary the colors and textures of the papers for different effects. Leave some space between the torn paper bits in which to add embroidery threads, as shown.

KEY

Time: less than 30 minutes

Techniques: paper mosaics, ribbon designs (looping), thread designs

Level of difficulty: advanced beginner

MATERIALS

Cell phone

Red-liner tape, 4" x 6" sheet

Wired ombre or multitoned ribbon

Two decorative buttons, one larger than the other

Decorative paper swatches, several colors

Narrow decorative braid or dimensional embroidery thread

Clear glass microbeads

Masking tape

Papers for Country French Phone.

Country French Phone.

❋ Coil the thread around the paper bits and press it into the exposed tape to secure it.

❋ Protect the openings in phone with masking tape. Place the phone in a shallow pan and pour clear glass microbeads over any remaining exposed tape. Swirl beads with fingertips to fully cover tape. Tap phone on its side to dislodge loose beads.

❋ To make ribbon flower appliqué, adhere a 1" square or circle or scrap of tape to center of phone back. Peel back top liner to expose sticky tape.

❋ Loop the wired ribbon to create petals, pressing the center of each petal into the tape to secure. When flower is complete, trim ribbon end, fold end under itself, and press into tape to hide it and prevent fraying.

❋ Apply a decorative button to the center of the flower with scrap tape. Here, a smaller button was applied over a larger button with additional scraps of tape.

STRUTTING YOUR STUFF

A few pair of basic shoes are all you need to create endless fashion statements when you choose to design your own look and change the design to suit your needs. Not only will you be strutting your stuff, but you will also be saving precious closet space and money, as well as avoiding the stress of having to hunt for the right fit time and time again.

Knockout Knock-offs

designed by Susan Zimmerman

Leafing through fashion magazines while at the hairdresser or a doctor's office is a great way to take in the latest trends and become inspired. Simple adornments can truly breathe new life into your wardrobe. It is especially satisfying to mimic the look of the times without having to pay high prices. The elegant design of these inexpensive evening shoes was inspired by a pair by a well-known international designer, featured in a magazine.

KEY

Time: 30 minutes

Techniques: basic embellishing, thread designs

Level of difficulty: beginner

MATERIALS

Black, closed-toe dress shoes

Red-liner tape, ⅛"-wide roll and ½" dots

Japan thread or other metallic embroidery thread

Rhinestones

Ultra-fine glitter

Prestrung sequins

Craft stick, awl, or tweezers

Metallic threads, rhinestones, and ultra-fine glitter add dazzle to these simple black pumps.

Another view of shoes, along with the fashion magazines that inspired their creation.

❋ Adhere three ½" tape dots to the front of each shoe (see photo for position). Next, apply a strip of tape down the back of the heel of each shoe. Apply a narrow piece of red-liner tape to the center front. Peel back the tape's protective liner as you go, to expose stickiness.

❋ Apply rhinestones down each heel by pressing them firmly into place on the tape.

❋ Apply a rhinestone to the center of each tape dot in front. Next, you can spiral metallic embroidery thread around the rhinestones until you have covered the entire tape dot. This is done by guiding the thread with one hand while pressing it into place with a craft stick, awl, or tweezers.

❋ Apply sequins to tape at center front of shoe.

❋ When you have completed your design, place the shoe over a paper plate and spoon ultra-fine glitter over the remaining exposed tape. Tap shoe on its side to dislodge excess glitter. Use a strip of tape wrapped around your fingers to dab areas on shoe that may have unwanted glitter. (This works like a lint roll.)

Party Shoes

designed by Susan Zimmerman

Those of you who tend to wear a simple black dress paired with bold accessories will have endless fun creating one-of-a-kind looks for the various events you attend. Here, faux jewels adorn basic black shoes, giving them a bejeweled look. Pair your new shoes with funky earrings, and you are good to go! Best of all, with all the attention on your accessories, you can get away with wearing that same black dress again and again.

❋ Apply tape to shoe straps and trim as desired. Peel back tape's top protective liner to expose its stickiness, one section at a time.

❋ Decorate each shoe with faux jewels by pressing them firmly into the tape.

❋ When you are pleased with your design, place the shoe in a shallow pan and spoon ultra-fine glitter over remaining exposed tape. Tap shoe on its side to dislodge excess glitter. Use a strip of tape wrapped around your fingers to help grab excess glitter (like a lint roll).

KEY

Time: up to 1 hour

Technique: basic embellishing

Level of difficulty: beginner

MATERIALS

Black shoes

Red-liner tape, ¼"-wide roll

Assorted faux pearls and rhinestones (or Lucite mosaic tiles)

Ultra-fine glitter

Terri O Tips

• Paper plates are the best thing to work with when using glitter, since glitter won't stick to them. This allows you to pour the excess back into the container for later use.

• Scour garage sales and flea markets for broken and old costume jewelry. They make beautiful gems for your projects.

These strappy shoes are trimmed with pearls, rhinestones, and other faux jewels.

MATERIALS

Slip-on sandals

Red-liner tape, 1"- and ¼"-wide rolls

Assorted fabric trims

High-tack craft glue such as Gem-Tac

Don't forget to
take care of your tootsies.
A pedicure is a must when
wearing these shoes.
After all, people
will be staring at your feet!
—T. O.

Vintage Fare Slip-ons

designed by Suzanne Chase

These sandals were adorned with miscellaneous beaded fabric trims that have become part of my cache of goodies over time. The variation in widths, styles, and colors is what makes the end result so attractive. If you don't have trims, visit a large fabric store, where you can buy assorted trims by the yard. With the right salesperson, you can usually purchase much less than an actual yard per trim.

❋ Apply strips of 1" red-liner tape over the entire top of the sandal. Overlap the tape, when needed, by peeling back the top liner on any strips already adhered to the sandal before adding the next strip. When taping is complete, peel back all top liners to fully expose tape.

❋ Adhere strips of assorted trim, one row at a time, across the top of the sandal by pressing them firmly into the tape. Since trims are fairly easy to position, you can press them lightly at first, check to make sure they are aligned nicely, and then press firmly to secure. As you start and end a new row, tuck the end of the trim under itself and press it firmly into the tape to create a no-sew seam and prevent fraying.

❋ To increase the durability of the sandals, apply a small dab of glue such as Gem-Tac, designed to bond porous and semiporous materials, to the trim ends.

❋ To give the sandal a more finished look, adhere a strip of ¼"-wide tape down each side and apply another narrow trim to cover over all the other trim ends.

Vintage trims.

Vintage Fare Slip-ons sport a variety of trims.

Terri O Tips

• The less flexible the shoe, the longer your creation will last. Avoid embellishing shoes with a lot of stretch in them.

• If you can't find vintage lace, make your own: Buy trims and then soak them in coffee or tea for that antiqued effect.

• Remember to stay out of the rain and away from the swimming pool with your sandals on, since the tape will lose its sticking power when wet.

KEY

Time: 1 hour, plus

Techniques: layering, trimming, paper mosaics, thread effects

Level of difficulty: intermediate

MATERIALS

Slip-on sandals

Red-liner tape, 1"- and ¼"-wide rolls

Origami papers

Lucite mosaic tiles

Assorted vintage trims

Thin ribbon

Metallic embroidery thread

Clear glass microbeads

Craft glue such as Gem-Tac

Supplies for Asian Flair Slip-ons.

Asian Flair Slip-ons

designed by Suzanne Chase

These slip-on sandals had a true transformation. I found them at a discount store; they were manufactured by a company that markets comfort over fashion. With the help of origami papers, mosaic tiles, and fabric trim, they were transformed into festive sandals, perfect for summer evenings out.

✳ Apply strips of 1" tape over the entire top of the sandal. Overlap the tape, when needed, by peeling back the top liner on any strips already adhered to the sandal before adding the next strip. When taping is complete, peel back all top liners to fully expose tape.

✳ Cut strips of origami paper and apply them to the exposed tape until the top of the sandal is fully covered.

✳ Apply another layer of tape over origami paper. Peel back top liners to expose stickiness.

✳ Create a design with mosaic tiles by pressing them firmly into the tape. Swirl embroidery threads in between the tiles for additional texture.

✳ Apply a double row of fanciful trims in coordinating colors to the top and bottom edges of the sandal, and add a single row along each side. The trims can all be the same for a more uniform look, or each one can vary for more of an artsy, one-of-a-kind look.

✳ To increase the durability of the sandals, apply a small dab of glue such as Gem-Tac, designed to bond porous and semiporous materials, to the trim ends.

✳ Adhere strips of tape around the edge of the base of the sandal, as well as over the brand name, and apply coordinating ribbon or trim.

✳ When your design is complete, place sandals in a shallow pan and pour in clear glass microbeads. This will cover the remaining exposed tape, while allowing the origami paper to show through.

Asian Flair Slip-ons. These bejeweled slip-ons are layered with origami paper and trim.

Breezy Slip-Ons

designed by Suzanne Chase

*B*reezy Mediterranean colors jazz up the pair of inexpensive sandals shown on page 74. The ombre ribbons used have graduated shades, and are just right for making ribbon roses.

✳ Apply strips of 1" tape over the entire top of the sandal. Overlap the tape, when needed, by peeling back the top liner on any strips already adhered to the sandal before adding the next strip. When taping is complete, peel back all top liners to fully expose tape.

✳ Tear and adhere bits of colorful paper to create your own color scheme on the top of the sandal. Here, a creamy taupe paper was used to soften the dark brown leather.

KEY

Time: 45 minutes per sandal

Techniques: paper mosaics, layering, ribbon designs, thread effects, trimming

Level of difficulty: intermediate

MATERIALS

Slip-on sandals

Red-liner tape, 1"- and ¼"-wide rolls

Colorful paper swatches

Wired ombre ribbon, ¾" wide

Embroidery threads

Assorted ribbons and trims

Small Lucite mosaic tiles

Clear glass microbeads

Breezy Slip-ons. Easy-to-make ribbon roses, along with mosaic tiles, embroidery threads, and pleated ribbons, spruce up these sandals.

✳ Once the paper scraps are covering the entire top of the shoe, add another layer of tape. Peel back the protective liner to expose stickiness.

✳ Apply strips of ¼" ribbon across the top of the sandal, creating stripes. Tuck each end of the ribbon under and press firmly into the tape to create a no-sew seam and prevent fraying. Pleat the ribbon along the bottom edge. Create ribbon roses by folding wired, 1"-wide ribbon in half, coiling it around itself, and pressing it into the red-liner tape along the front of the sandal.

✳ Add strips of ¼" red-liner tape to the ribbon stripes so that curled and coiled embroidery thread can be layered over the ribbon. On the ribbon stripe just above the row of roses, adhere small Lucite mosaic tiles.

✳ When the design is complete, place the sandal in a shallow container and pour clear glass microbeads over remaining exposed tape to fully cover.

✳ Adhere a strip of decorative trim along base of sandal with ¼" tape.

MORE ACCESSORIZING

The perfect accessory will always pull your look together. You can make one to stand out or blend right in, depending on the occasion and your mood. Cuff bracelets, baseball caps, and barrettes are jazzed up in this chapter, to show you ways to help you express your style or mood.

Dapper Headbands

designed by Suzanne Chase

Thank goodness men's necktie styles constantly change. One year short and wide is in; the next year, narrow and long. As a result, men often have oodles of ties in their closet that they no longer wear. We encourage you to root out these old ties from your man's closet (any man will do, e.g., your husband, brother, father, boyfriend, neighbor). Be sure to get his permission, however. Neckties offer a gorgeous array of colors, textures, and patterns. Add them to your embellishment treasures. Ironically enough, you may even get back some of the ties you gave as gifts. Here, we show how simple headbands are transformed into handsome, luxurious headgear.

KEY

Time: 15 to 20 minutes

Techniques: wrapping

Level of difficulty: intermediate

MATERIALS

Plain, 1"-wide headband

Old necktie

Red-liner tape, ¾" roll

High-tack glue such as Gem-Tac

An assortment of headbands, made by wrapping basic headbands with men's neckties.

Another view of headbands.

✳ Apply a strip of tape lengthwise to underside of headband. Peel back the tape's protective liner to expose stickiness.

✳ Starting with the narrow end of the tie and one end of the headband, begin wrapping the headband, overlapping each wrap slightly until the headband is almost completely covered. The strip of tape applied to the inside of the headband will secure the tie as you wrap it around the headband. Trim off the tie end, leaving a bit of extra to tuck under, and press onto the tape to hide raw edge. For best results, cut out some of the tie's lining on the trimmed end to make it less bulky for tucking under.

✳ For added durability, we recommend adding a dab of high-tack glue such as Gem-Tac to the end of the tie when tucking it under, to firmly secure it.

Terri O Tips

• Almost any leftover piece of fabric will work for a headband. It just has to be long enough. Test-wrap it before you tape it to make sure you'll have enough.

• If you find your headband keeps slipping off your head when it is covered in silk, try adding a thin strip of felt inside with ¼" red-liner tape.

Barrettes, embellished with mosaic tiles, fabric, trim, and buttons.

Sporty Cap

designed by Suzanne Chase

KEY

Time: 30 minutes

Technique: ribbon designs

Level of difficulty: advanced beginner

MATERIALS

Baseball cap

Red-liner tape, 1"-wide roll

Assorted ribbon and clothing trim, including some ¼" wide or narrower

Buttons

Ribbon, trim, and buttons bring this denim cap to life.

$\mathcal{B}$aseball caps have become true fashion statements for both men and women. They can be worn to display a fashionable sports team logo or to emulate the hat style of a favorite rock star. Headgear communicates your personal sense of style. Here, we show you how to create your own unique cap design. Who knows? Maybe one of your creations will become the next look to emulate.

❈ Cover peak of cap with strips of red-liner tape. You can overlap the tape, if necessary, by peeling the protective liner off the strip you have already laid down and then applying the new strip over it. When peak is completely covered in tape, peel off any protective liners to fully expose tape.

Terri O Tips

- *Have fun twisting and turning the ribbon. Try to create your own unique technique.*
- *Have a fun event to go to? Plan on making matching caps for everyone! Some ladies I know made matching caps for their scrapbooking club.*
- *If you know that someone is in the Red Hat Society, surprise her with a funky red cap.*

With an assortment of different textured and colored ribbons and trims, embellish the peak, one row at a time, starting with the edge of the peak and working in. Here, three different thin trims (¼" wide or less) were applied and then a wider velvet ribbon was zigzagged to fill in the remaining exposed tape (for more information, see Zigzagging on page 23).

Adhere buttons with scraps of tape for added dimension and to give the zigzagging a more finished look. Apply another strip of tape just above the brim, and stick a beaded clothing trim to the tape. Tuck under the ends of the beaded trim and press into the tape to create seams and prevent fraying.

Romantic Rose Cuff

designed by Christina Santangelo

A simple cuff bracelet can be transformed into a gorgeous personal statement to match your every mood or outfit. Our favorite bracelets to use are metal-reinforced so they can bend around your wrist. However, cuff bracelets can also be found in Lucite and other plastics, as well as stiff metal. They are typically available in discount and mass-market stores, as well as various clothing boutiques. All you need is a surface ¾" wide or wider to create a masterpiece or two or three.

KEY

Time: 40 minutes

Techniques: paper mosaics, layering, ribbon designs

Level of difficulty: beginner to intermediate

MATERIALS

1"-wide or wider leather cuff bracelets

Red-liner tape, ¾"-wide roll

Pretty paper scraps, assorted colors

1" wired rose ombre ribbon

Assorted faux cabochons and small plastic mosaic tiles

Clear glass microbeads

The ribbon used is called ombre (meaning "shadow" in French), recognized by its hand-dyed, multicolored look.

Apply a strip of ¾" tape to outside of bracelet, covering it lengthwise (from one end of the cuff to the other). Peel back tape's protective liner to expose its stickiness.

Tear bits of paper in assorted colors and adhere directly onto the tape to create your first layer of embellishment.

* Next, apply another layer of tape over the bracelet, covering the paper mosaic design. Peel back protective liner to expose sticky tape.

* Fold a 1" ombre ribbon in half and curl it around itself to create a rosebud; trim off any excess. Place rosebud in center of bracelet and press into place, tucking under the ribbon ends, and press onto tape to hide and secure them. Continue to decorate cuff by applying cabochons or small mosaic tiles to both sides of ribbon rose.

* Once you are pleased with your design, hold the cuff bracelet over a shallow pan and pour clear glass microbeads over any remaining exposed tape to fully cover tape. Gently press beads into place. Tap project on its side to dislodge any excess beads.

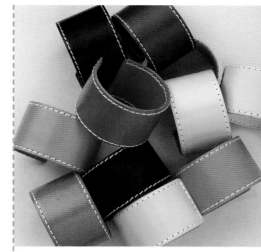

Cuffs before decoration.

Romantic Rose Cuff.

Other cuffs, decorated with assorted goodies, some layered over images such as photos or scrapbook papers.

ACCENTING YOUR CLOTHING

Think how much fun it will be to change the look of what's in your wardrobe on a whim! With red-liner tape, you can go from frumpy to funky in just minutes. No more wasting money on special-occasion outfits, when you can just transform your basics for any evening out.

The embellished item can be laundered using one of the home "dry cleaning" systems sold at grocery stores, designed to work in your dryer. Unfortunately, the item should not be machine-washed or submerged in water, since red-liner tape loses its sticking power when wet. Many professional dry cleaning systems are wet systems, too. However, as another option, we suggest simply pulling off the trim when you need to launder the garment, so you can create a new look the next time. After all, it will only take minutes to redecorate.

KEY

Time: as little as 15 minutes

Techniques: trimming, thread effects, ribbon designs

Level of difficulty: beginner

MATERIALS

Red-liner tape, ¾"- and ¼"-wide rolls

Assorted trims, ribbons, dimensional embroidery threads, etc.

Optional: sequins, rhinestones, pearls, etc.

Clear glass microbeads (if embellishing with decorative threads)

Trimming Clothing

Instantly add decorative trim to clothing for any occasion by applying it with red-liner tape. You can jazz up anything from jeans and T-shirts to festive skirts, dresses, and jackets. As for the trimmings, you have plenty of choices, such as ribbon, embroidery thread, lace, prestrung sequins, and fabric trim.

❋ Apply a strip of red-liner tape to the clothing you want to embellish, in a width that corresponds to the trim you will be using. The tape can be applied to the front of the garment or hidden underneath near the hem. Once tape is applied, start to peel back the tape's top protective liner to reveal its stickiness.

❋ Apply trim by adhering it directly onto tape. Don't forget to tuck trim ends under and press them into the tape to prevent fraying and to create neat, no-sew seams.

Left to right, starting at top:

1 *Metallic thread and faux jewels on jeans.*

2 *Silk flowers and ribbon decorate a pants hem.*

3 *Vintage fabric trim was applied to this T-shirt.*

4 *Zigzagged ribbon and decorative buttons trim a jeans jacket.*

5 *Playful feather trim decorates this sleeve.*

6 *A touch of ribbon and funky beaded trim adorn the bottom of a jeans jacket.*

7 *Edge of jacket is enlivened by ribbon and beaded fringe.*

Time: 30 minutes to 2 hours

Technique: embellishing

Level of difficulty: intermediate

MATERIALS

Artwork or image

Printer fabric sheets for image transfer

Red-liner tape, 8" x 10" sheet

Assorted embellishments (e.g., old ties, trims, buttons; the more, the merrier)

Clear glass microbeads

Terri O Tips

• Embellish around any accidental creases you may have created when taping over the image.

• To reuse your appliqués, save the tape sheet's discarded top liner so you have a place to stick your appliqués between uses. You can reapply fresh strips of tape on the appliqué's back, once the tape starts to lose its sticking power (from multiple applications).

Appliqués

Create real conversation pieces by designing your own clothing appliqués. These wonderful appliqués are expressive and impressive-looking, yet so easy to make. They can be designed to be playful or sophisticated. Try adding a sweet touch to an outfit one day and making a very dramatic statement the next. The look will vary depending on the image you choose and its size, as well as the type and amount of embellishing you do. Appliqués can be adhered to your clothing with strips of red-liner tape, or you can sew Velcro strips on the appliqués and on the clothing, so that you can remove the appliqués before laundering the clothes.

A child's artwork was the source of the peacock appliqué.

❊ Pick an image to embellish, and photocopy it onto a printer fabric sheet (see page 29 for more details). Almost any image will work, although images with strong colors, high contrast, and defined areas of interest work best for mixed-media embellishing (see Sources of Images on page 16 for more ideas). If you don't have (or can't find) fabric sheets for your printer, you can use ordinary copy paper to copy an image, or you can even use the original image on paper. The finished appliqué won't be quite as sturdy as if it were created on a fabric sheet, but it will be fine for most uses.

✳ Once you have your image on fabric (or paper if you chose this method), it is time to cover it in red-liner tape. To do this, trim a sheet of tape to fit over the entire image. Place the transferred image on the table in front of you. Then peel back one side of the tape's backing and line up the exposed tape edges with the corresponding edges of the image. Press tape edges onto the edges of the image. Slowly peel back the rest of the backing, pressing the tape sheet onto the image as you go, until it is fully covered. Using a credit card, brayer, or similar item, smooth out the tape over the image. Now you can peel back the tape's top protective liner to expose its stickiness.

✳ If you get air bubbles caught under the tape, just prick them with a pin. Reapply the plastic top sheet from the red-liner tape, and push out the air.

✳ Lay out an assortment of goodies from your craft supply cache. Start applying all those goodies to the exposed tape, using the image as your design template. Depending on your mood, you can add a little bit of embellishment and let a lot of the image show through or cover up a lot (or all) of the image and basically recreate the image with embellishments.

✳ Once you have embellished the image to your liking, place the item in a shallow pan and pour clear glass microbeads over remaining exposed tape. Swirl with fingertips to fully cover tape. The appliqué can be applied to your clothing by tacking it down with additional tape.

Terri O Tips

• For larger projects, which require an 8" x 10" sheet of tape, once you have exposed the tape, use the top liner to cover up one area while you are working on another. That way, you can work in sections and keep your project clear of stuff you don't want.

• Your creations can be applied to just about anything. Try decorating a pillow, quilt square, or notebook cover.

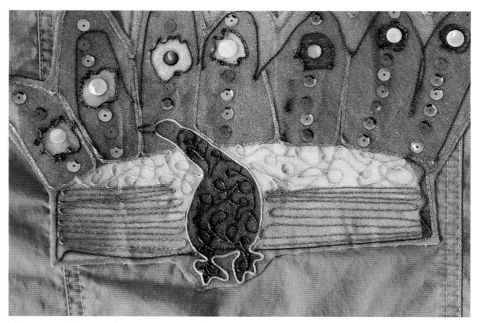

The peacock artwork was decorated with faux jewels, embroidery thread, trims, and sequins.

The Infamous Jacket That Brought Us Together

Appliqué was taken to the extreme on this jeans jacket, created as a promotional piece for a craft industry trade show. Here is the jacket that caught Terri O's eye at the show and initiated our relationship. Each panel of the back of the jacket was decorated with a different old-world style textile pattern. An assortment of metallic embroidery threads and vintage Lucite cabochons were applied to accent the images. Vintage trim was used to cover over the areas in between each image, creating the look of a crazy quilt. Although this jacket is truly a work of art, it is a bit stiff to wear every day. For most of us, creating an 8" × 10" appliqué that is removable will work best—unless, of course, you believe in fashion over comfort!

The appliquéd jacket from the crafts show.

GETTING NOTICED AT THE OFFICE

Adding your personal flair to your desk accessories will ensure that you get noticed. You can easily dress up staplers, frames, and other dull office equipment to express your style or mood and to show off your favorite family members and pets. (You also won't have to look too far to see who took your stapler.) These make great co-worker and teacher gifts.

Fancy Calculators

designed by Suzanne Chase

Who says a calculator has to look technical and uninspiring? Here, a photo die-cut of a beautiful butterfly adds flair to the cover of an otherwise dull-looking office tool. Colorful ribbons and other scraps coordinate with the butterfly image for extra pizzazz (photo on p. 86).

Calculator with Cover

✳ Tack butterfly image onto the cover of your calculator with red-liner tape.

✳ Apply strips of tape to cover of calculator, over butterfly, overlapping when necessary. To do this, peel the top liner off the strip already on the calculator before placing the next strip over it. When calculator is completely taped, peel back the remaining protective liners to expose the tape's stickiness.

✳ Tear bits of scrapbook paper and adhere them around butterfly to frame it. Next, outline butterfly with embroidery threads, guiding the threads with one hand while pressing them into place with the other. Adhere rhinestones to wings and head.

✳ Apply ¼"-wide roll of tape around frame of calculator and decorate with ribbon. Here, strips of ribbon were adhered on the sides, while ribbon was zigzagged on the top and bottom.

KEY

Time: 30 minutes

Techniques: embellishing images, ribbon designs, paper mosaics, layering

Level of difficulty: advanced beginner

MATERIALS

Calculator with cover

Small calculator

Red-liner tape, ¾" roll

Butterfly die-cut or other photo of butterfly

Scrapbook paper scraps

Coordinating ribbon

Dimensional embroidery thread

Colored rhinestones

Clear glass microbeads

When design work is complete, place calculator in a shallow pan and pour clear glass microbeads over any remaining exposed tape to fully cover tape. Tap project on its side to dislodge excess beads.

The cover of a calculator was decorated with bits of scrap paper, a photo die-cut of a butterfly, and other embellishments.

Terri O Tips

- *Die-cuts are paper shapes that have been precut. Many have pretty designs. They work very well for layering and embellishing. It's easy to embellish the details on these pretty papers with threads and beads.*
- *Red-liner tape is very forgiving, since you can layer additional embellishing over mistakes to cover them up!*

Small Calculator

Apply a strip of ¾" tape across top of calculator. Peel back protective liner to expose tape.

Adhere strips of ⅛" ribbon to top and bottom of exposed red-liner tape and then smoosh bright-colored ribbon along the center of the tape.

Green ribbon and hot-pink ribbon were applied to the top of a calculator.

Clever Clips and Clip Box

designed by Sue Zimmerman

When it comes to gift giving, choosing things for your coworkers can be really challenging. Why not make them a set of clever clips? They're perfect for just about anyone. It's easy and quick to do, and your coworker will know that you took the time to create something unique just for her. Include a nifty box to keep them in.

KEY

Time: up to 10 minutes for each clip

Techniques: basic embellishing, thread effects, trimming, layering

Level of difficulty: beginner

MATERIALS

Binder clips

Red-liner tape, ¼"- and ¾"-wide rolls

Decorative metallic threads

Iridescent cabochons or other faux jewels

Beaded fringe

Ribbon

Clear glass microbeads

Plastic storage box for clips

Binder clips were jazzed up by applying mosaic tiles, beads, faux jewels, and embroidery threads. The decorated container has coordinated colors.

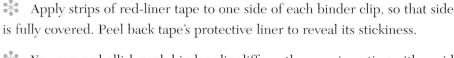

❋ Apply strips of red-liner tape to one side of each binder clip, so that side is fully covered. Peel back tape's protective liner to reveal its stickiness.

❋ You can embellish each binder clip differently, experimenting with a wide variety of goodies, or you can create a themed set for someone special. Here, we used faux jewels and dimensional embroidery threads. The cabochons are simply placed onto the exposed tape and pressed into place. The embroidery threads are applied by drawing with one hand and pressing into place with the other.

❋ When you are pleased with your design, place the clips in a shallow pan and pour glitter, clear glass microbeads, or colored microbeads over remaining exposed tape to fully cover. You can tap the clips on their side to dislodge excess beads.

❋ Decorate the storage box with beaded fringe, ribbon, and faux jewels as shown.

Closeup of binder clips.

Beachy Frame

designed by Suzanne Chase

Next time you go shell-seeking at the beach, save your favorite finds to perk up a basic photo frame. You can put an image of your family in your new vacation keepsake and display it at the office. Use it as a reminder of stress-free, relaxing times to focus on momentarily when things get hectic around you. If you don't find the right assortment of shells while away on vacation, you can always purchase some at a crafts store.

KEY

Time: 45 minutes

Technique: basic embellishing

Level of difficulty: beginner

MATERIALS

Frame, 1" wide or wider

Red-liner tape, 1"-wide roll

Assorted shells

Buttons, faux-pearl cabochons, sea glass, or sand (optional)

Clear glass microbeads

This frame was decorated with shells collected by our family on a recent vacation. Faux-pearl cabochons were mixed in to add extra interest.

Collecting mementos from a vacation can be so much fun. When I look back at those precious moments, it puts a smile on my face. —T. O.

KEY

Time: 30 minutes

Techniques: basic embellishing and wrapping

Level of difficulty: beginner

MATERIALS

Decorate-a-mug kit

Red-liner tape, 8" x 10" sheet

Thin textured yarn

Small scrapbooking quotes and letter tiles or tokens

Translucent quote tiles from the scrapbooking aisle, used for mug.

✳ Apply strips of 1" tape to fully cover the frame. You can overlap the tape, if necessary, by peeling the protective liner off one strip before applying the next strip. When frame is covered, peel back all protective liners to fully expose tape.

✳ Apply shells around the frame in desired pattern. Shell buttons, faux-pearl cabochons and other "beachy" items can be incorporated.

✳ When you are pleased with your design, place the frame in a shallow pan and pour clear glass microbeads over any remaining exposed tape. Swirl with fingertips to fully cover tape. Tap project on its side to dislodge loose beads.

Cozy Mug

designed by Terri O

Here is a twist on those decorate-a-mug kits designed for kids to color in and use at the table. Instead of coloring the insert in, cover it with tape and embellish it with whatever you wish. If you have more than one idea in mind, just use the insert as a template and cut out a bunch of inserts to decorate in many different ways. That way, you can switch your mug motif anytime you please.

✳ Peel backing off red-liner tape sheet and adhere it to mug's paper insert. Trim tape sheet down to the size of the paper insert. Peel off tape's top protective liner to expose its stickiness.

✳ Place scrapbooking quote tiles and lettering as desired, by adhering them directly onto the tape. Remember, the cup is curved, so the smaller the better when it comes to tiles or metal quotes.

❋ Next, fill in the remaining exposed tape with rows of textured yarn. Do this by guiding the yarn with one hand while pressing it into place with the other. Work around the tiles with the yarn as you go. Feel free to cut yarn (pressing end into tape) so that you can start up in a different area, if desired. When you have finished winding yarn around all remaining exposed tape areas, press the yarn and tiles against the tape to fully secure.

Novelty yarns and scrapbooking tokens were applied with tape to a mug insert paper.

MATERIALS

Day planner

Red-liner tape, two 8" x 10" sheets

Textured paper for mats

5" x 7" school photo

Scrapbooking fibers

Novelty shaped buttons

Glass mosaic stones

Clear glass microbeads

Dimensional embroidery thread

Supplies for Day Planner.

My Hero Day Planner

designed by Terri O

If you are a working mom, here is a fun way to spruce up a dull day planner with a photo of your little hero at home. You can jazz up the photo with all kinds of scrapbooking supplies, and by doing so, bring a little creative energy and inspiration to the office. You should have seen the smile on my little guy's face when he saw this. It made him feel good to know I was proudly showing him off!

✳ Trim photo and cut two mats from textured paper to go behind it, one smaller than the other, to fit on the cover of your day planner. Make the mats wider and taller than the photo, to leave a border around it.

✳ Adhere a tape sheet, trimmed to size, to the cover of the day planner by peeling off the tape's backing and placing it directly onto the day planner. Next, remove the tape's top protective liner to expose its stickiness. Adhere the larger mat to cover of day planner, being careful to line it up properly before pressing it into place.

✳ Tack photo to the smaller mat with scrap tape; then tack the matted photo to the larger mat on the cover of the day planner with additional scraps. Cover smaller mat with 1"-wide strips of tape, or whatever width you need. Pull off tape's top protective liner to expose its stickiness. Decorate mat with novelty buttons and small mosaic stones by applying them directly onto tape on the mat. Add dimensional thread around inner mat border by guiding it with one hand while pressing it into place with the other.

✳ When you are pleased with your design, place the day planner in a shallow pan and pour clear glass microbeads over remaining exposed tape to fully cover tape. Tap on side to shake off any excess beads.

A school photo decorates this Day Planner, along with textured papers and novelty buttons.

Terri O Tips

• If you don't want to use an original photo, make a color copy instead. In either case, you may want to put a clear transparent sheet over your photo or laminate it to protect it, especially if you use your day planner as much as I do.

• This project is a great gift idea for dads and grandparents. Get the kids involved to help you design and decorate.

STANDING OUT ON VACATION

Packing for your next vacation can be made easy and fun by choosing only the basics and then sticking all kinds of embellishments on them while away. Transform sunhats and your beach bag daily, and incorporate your vacation memorabilia into your outfit and accessories.

KEY

Time: 30 minutes to 1 hour

Techniques: trimming, ribbon designs, thread effects, basic embellishing, layering

Level of difficulty: advanced beginner

MATERIALS

1½" grosgrain ribbon

Red-liner tape, 1"-wide roll

Dimensional embroidery thread

Assorted plastic and glass cabochons

Clear glass microbeads

Decorative wrapping paper

Liquid seam sealant or clear nail polish

Measuring tape or ruler

The ribbon was embellished with wrapping paper, Lucite jewelry cabochons, embroidery thread, and mosaic tiles.

Showy Sunhat

designed by Suzanne Chase

Just because you need to protect yourself from the sun doesn't mean you have to look unfashionable. Perk up a plain sunhat with a strip of wide ribbon, embellished with anything from mosaic tiles to seashells. Sometimes it's hard to stop at one ribbon look, so don't. You can make a bunch to match your different vacation wear; after all, they aren't expensive to make and tuck easily into your suitcase.

✳ Measure the circumference of your hat where the ribbon will go. Cut a ribbon that length plus 12" so that the ribbon is long enough to knot and have decorative dangling ends.

✳ Adhere a strip of 1" red-liner tape lengthwise down the center of the ribbon, starting 6" in and ending 6" before the second end of the ribbon. Peel back the tape's protective liner to expose its stickiness.

✳ Decorate the ribbon with all sorts of goodies. In the sample shown, a decorative wrapping paper was cut into a 1"-wide strip and adhered to the tape. A second layer of red-liner tape was applied on top of it. Once the top liner was peeled back, the strip was embellished with buttons, plastic jewels, mosaic cabochons, and dimensional embroidery threads by pressing them gently into place. The embroidery threads were applied by guiding them with one hand while pressing them into place with the other.

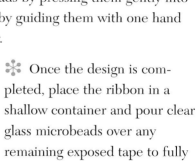

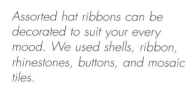

Assorted hat ribbons can be decorated to suit your every mood. We used shells, ribbon, rhinestones, buttons, and mosaic tiles.

✳ Once the design is completed, place the ribbon in a shallow container and pour clear glass microbeads over any remaining exposed tape to fully cover.

✳ Wrap the ribbon around the base of the sunhat and knot it. Trim the ribbon ends and apply liquid seam sealant to the tips to prevent fraying. Clear nail polish also can be used.

Terri O Tips

• Hats are in. Do one up and flaunt your creativity.

• Make up a few different colors of ribbon in advance, to match your different swimsuits and sundresses.

• Be sure the ribbon is slightly wider than the red-liner tape. That way, you have nice clean ribbon edges.

Time: less than 1 hour

Techniques: trimming, wrapping, ribbon designs, basic embellishing

Level of difficulty: intermediate

MATERIALS

Beach bag

Red-liner tape, ¼"- and 1"-wide rolls

Beaded fringe

Wired ombre ribbon (here, red-peach-green), ¾" wide

Grosgrain ribbon, 1" wide

Mulberry-paper roses

Magenta satin ribbon, ¼" wide

See how an inexpensive bag can become priceless! —T. O.

Rosy Beach Bag

designed by Suzanne Chase

Flowers, whether plucked from the floral section of your local crafts store or made quickly by hand with wired ribbon, are perfect for jazzing up a beach bag. You can go big and flashy or tiny and dainty, depending on your mood. Here, mulberry-paper flowers, designed for paper crafts, are paired with handmade ribbon roses. Additional ribbon designs and beaded trim were added to make a real statement.

Super-easy handmade ribbon roses, beaded fringe, and paper flowers adorn this inexpensive beach tote.

❋ Adhere a 1"-wide strip of red-liner tape around one side of the bag at the top opening. Next, adhere a strip of ¼" red-liner tape just below it. Remove protective liners from tape as you go, to expose its stickiness.

❋ Embellish the bag to your liking with ribbons, mulberry-paper flowers, and trim. Here, green grosgrain ribbon was zigzagged across the 1" tape strip. Beaded fringe was applied just below the grosgrain ribbon onto the ¼" tape strip. Another strip of ¼" tape was applied on top of the beaded trim, and ¼" magenta satin ribbon was pleated across it.

❋ Apply mulberry-paper roses to the grosgrain ribbon with tape scraps. The paper roses were interspersed with handmade ribbon roses, created by folding wired ombre ribbon in half and then coiling the ribbon around itself to create a rosebud, on our model. Press each rosebud onto a scrap piece of red-liner tape to hold it in place. Since the tape is double-sided, the other side was used to adhere the rosebud to the bag.

❋ Adhere a strip of the ¼"-wide red-liner tape lengthwise to the inside of each handle.

❋ Starting at the base of the handle, wrap the ombre ribbon around and around, overlapping slightly as you go, until the entire handle is covered. Tuck ends of ribbon under and press them firmly into the tape to create a no-sew seam.

KEY

Time: 45 minutes to 1 hour

Techniques: paper mosaics, layering, image embellishing

Level of difficulty: intermediate

MATERIALS

Travel journal

Red-liner tape, 8" x 10" sheet

Clear glass microbeads

Scrapbooking papers

Metal charms

Embroidery thread

Assorted yarns or scrap-booking fibers

Clear plastic magnifying page pebble

Dreamy Travel Journal

designed by Terri O

If you carry a travel journal to record all the sights you've seen and food you've tasted, consider decorating the cover with assorted scrapbooking goodies. There is a huge assortment of travel-themed supplies available, including stickers, die-cuts, quotes, and papers. That way, in addition to keeping copious notes on the inside of your journal, you can communicate something about yourself on the outside.

❋ Tear out all of the papers to the shapes you want and lay them out first, so you can place them exactly where you want them. If the papers don't fit, just tear them to size. We used four different paper patterns, one for each corner of the book cover, in our model.

❋ When tearing paper, consider the direction of the tear. If you tear away from you, you will make a clean tear, while if you tear in the other direction, you will create a white edge. To see what I mean, tear the paper towards you and then away from you, and note the difference.

❋ Adhere your background papers to the book with scraps of red-liner tape. Make sure your edges are lined up well.

❋ Notice the size of your cover. We kept our paper slightly smaller than the size of the journal's front cover so we would have room for a border.

❋ Cover the entire journal front with an 8" **x** 10"

Supplies for Dreamy Travel Journal.

sheet of tape, or whatever size you need. Large sheets of tape can be tricky. Peel back the top of the tape's backing sheet about ½" and adhere the tape to the top of the cover. Then gently peel the backing sheet away as you smooth down the tape sheet to the bottom of your cover. I used a credit card as a smoothing tool to keep the air bubbles out.

✳ Embellish some parts of the designs on the paper with embroidery threads. Add a plastic quote pebble (found in scrapbooking aisle) or clear glass mosaic stone to magnify other areas. We also added a metal charm with a quote on it.

✳ When decorating is complete, place the journal in a shallow pan and cover the remaining exposed tape with clear glass microbeads, which allow the image underneath to show through. Tap on the side to remove any excess.

Terri O Tips

• *Buying paper in a collage kit makes it easier to coordinate your colors. This takes all of the guesswork out for some and all the fun out for others. To each his own.*

• *Large glass pebbles (domes) are great for magnifying things. Find something interesting and magnify it.*

A collage of papers and scrapbooking tags, thread, charms, and ribbon was adhered to this journal.

PERSONALIZING YOUR WEDDING

A wedding is the most meaningful occasion you can personalize. There are many opportunities to express yourself in the event's details. From bridal accessories, to party favors, to keepsakes, you can make the moment truly yours. Do it yourself or, better yet, offer a crafts night or workshop for your friends and family to help create these objects and give folks a chance to get to know each other.

KEY

Time: 45 minutes to 1 hour

Techniques: ribbon designs, wrapping, thread effects

Level of difficulty: intermediate

MATERIALS

Satin-finish bag with flap

Red-liner tape, 8" x 10" sheet and 1"-wide roll

Antique lace ribbon

Assorted ribbon, including wide cream-colored ribbon and ribbon for handle

Shell buttons

Narrow decorative braid (32-strand)

Clear glass microbeads or glitter

Ancestry Bag

designed by Suzanne Chase

My grandmother's goodies, boxed up in my basement since we sold her house, were used to decorate a basic satin-finish handbag. Some of the boxes were full of memories and valuables to be passed on; other boxes contained odds and ends that I knew I would never use but had trouble parting with because they were handsome, often handmade, and reminiscent of yesteryear. I found some wonderful old lace ribbon that I used, along with some complementary supplies, to create a wonderful new keepsake.

❋ Cover the flap of the bag with red-liner tape by trimming a tape sheet to size and adhering it to the flap; or use tape scraps if you want, overlapping the pieces when necessary. This is done by adhering one piece, then peeling back its top liner, and adhering the next piece. When the flap is fully covered, peel back any remaining protective liners to expose sticky tape.

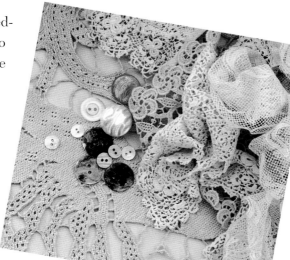

Supplies for Ancestry Bag.

✳ Apply a strip of shell buttons across the bottom of the flap and then zigzag embroidery threads in between the buttons to create a textured filler. Next, curl and coil a row of cream-colored ribbon coils across the front of the flap, just above the buttons. This is done by coiling the ribbon around itself, similar to the way in which ribbon roses are created (see page 25), and then pressing the coils into the tape. After creating a coil, the ribbon is curled in the opposite direction and the next coil is started. The coils should gradually increase in size, so that the largest coil is in the center of the row, and should then taper down again (see photo).

✳ Smoosh bits of antique lace all around any remaining undecorated areas of the flap (see photo).

✳ If any exposed tape remains once you have decorated the bag, place it over a shallow container and pour beads (or glitter) over the remaining exposed tape to fully cover.

✳ Adhere a strip of 1" tape to the inside of the bag's handle, and peel the top liner back to expose the tape.

✳ Wrap decorative ribbon around the handle to fully cover. Start by tucking approximately ⅛" of the ribbon end under and pressing it into the tape to create a no-sew seam and prevent fraying. When finished wrapping, trim the other end, leaving enough ribbon to tuck the end under.

Terri O Tips

• If you don't have antique lace but like the look, you can tea-dye store-bought cotton lace. Brew tea in a small amount of water and then soak the lace in tea until it reaches the desired color. Squeeze out excess liquid and let dry.

• Red-liner tape won't ruin anything you stick it to, so go ahead and use Grandma's antique lace to add something old to your ensemble.

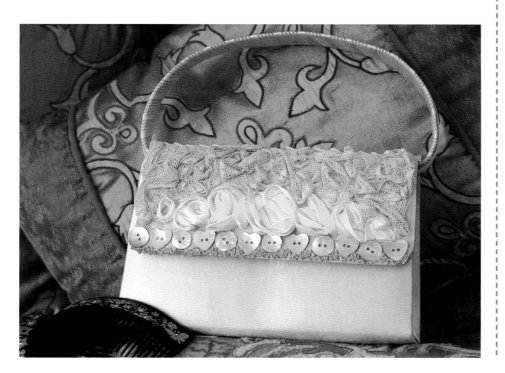

Grandmother's old lace, ribbon, and buttons were adhered to this simple satin bag to create a new family heirloom.

KEY

Time: 30 minutes

Technique: ribbon designs, layering

Level of difficulty: beginner

MATERIALS

Metal cuff or other bracelet form

Red-liner tape, ¾"- and ¼"-wide rolls

Antique lace

Beaded trim

Shell buttons

Small glass mosaic tiles, rhinestones, or cabochons

Craft knife or scissors

Clear glass microbeads

Something Borrowed, Something Blue Bracelet

designed by Suzanne Chase

A stunning bracelet was created from something old, something new, something borrowed, and something blue. You can create a similar one by starting with a stiff bracelet form that has a flat surface area to embellish.

❋ Apply strips of red-liner tape to fully cover bracelet form on outside. You can overlap tape strips if necessary by peeling top liner off of a strip already adhered to bracelet and then applying the next strip, overlapping it. When bracelet is fully covered, peel all remaining top liners off to expose sticky tape.

❋ Apply embellishments to your liking. When using trims and lace, it is fun to layer them. Here, a layer of lace was adhered to the entire bracelet. The ends of the lace were tucked under and pressed into the tape to create no-sew seams.

Supplies for bracelet.

❋ Adhere a strip of ¾" tape down the center of the bracelet (on top of the lace), and apply ¼"-wide red-liner tape above and below it. Peel top liners off at this time or one at a time, as you go.

❋ Adhere beaded trim down the center strip of tape, tuck each end of the trim under, and press into the tape to create no-sew seams. This also helps to prevent fraying. Alternate shell buttons and small mosaic tiles on the edges of the bracelet, by pressing them gently into the tape.

❋ Once your design work is complete, place the bracelet in a shallow pan and pour microbeads over any remaining exposed tape to fully cover tape. Secure embellishments by lightly squeezing bracelet all around. Tap cuff on its side to dislodge any excess beads.

New and old embellishments combine on this sentimental cuff.

Bridesmaid Headbands

designed by Suzanne Chase

You can make a plain headband into a perfect hair ornament simply by wrapping it with lace. Why not have your bridesmaids decorate these headbands to express their personal styles?

❋ Adhere ¾" red-liner tape lengthwise to inside of headband. Peel back tape's protective liner to expose its stickiness.

❋ Starting on the inside of one end of the headband, begin wrapping lace ribbon around it. Slightly overlap each wrap to ensure that entire headband is covered.

KEY

Time: 10 to 15 minutes

Techniques: wrapping, layering

Level of difficulty: beginner

MATERIALS

Plain white or cream headband

Red-liner tape, ¾"- and ¼"-wide rolls

Lace ribbon

Decorative trim, narrower than headband

Supplies for Bridesmaid Headband.

Adhere a ¼"-wide strip of tape down the center of the headband, over the lace. Peel back the tape's top liner to expose it. Apply decorative trim down center of headband by pressing into place. Firmly press trim ends into tape to prevent fraying.

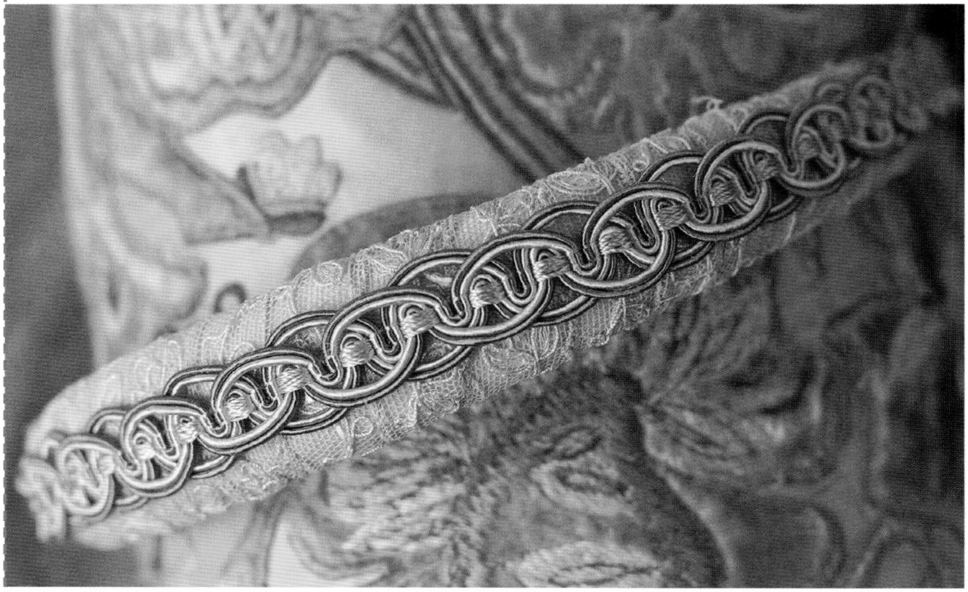

A plain headband was purchased at a crafts store and then embellished by wrapping lace around it and adhering decorative trim.

Flower-Girl Fun

designed by Madeleine, Caroline, and Olivia Chase

These adorable purses were decorated by my three daughters (ages 7, 8, and 8), who were thrilled to add a personal touch to their flower-girl outfits. The bags were inexpensively purchased at a discount store. We spread the embellishments out on a table and I encouraged the girls to dig in. I helped with the thread writing; the rest came from their unique inspirations.

KEY

Time: up to 1 hour

Techniques: embellishing, ribbon designs

Level of difficulty: beginner

MATERIALS

Child's handbag

Red-liner tape, ¼" and ¾" rolls and dots

Assorted ribbons, rhinestones, artificial flowers, sewing notions, etc., including ¼" ribbon for handle

Metallic embroidery threads (32-strand)

Clear glass microbeads

Apply strips of tape in varying widths, as well as tape dots, to handbag wherever you want to embellish. Peel back top liners to reveal sticky tape as you go.

Decorate with all sorts of trims and embellishments, starting with the larger items first and ending with the smallest.

❋ Write "Flower Girl" in embroidery thread by guiding the threads with one hand while pressing them into place with the other, if you wish. Secure all thread work by replacing the top liner of the tape over the taped area and pressing threads firmly into place.

❋ Place purse in a shallow container and pour microbeads over remaining exposed tape to fully cover tape.

❋ Apply a strip of ¼" tape lengthwise to the inside of purse handles. Peel back top liner.

❋ Wrap ¼" ribbon around entire handle by starting at the base and working your way around and around, slightly overlapping each wrap to fully cover handle. Tuck ribbon ends under and press into place to create a finished edge.

These flower-girl purses were individualized with an assortment of novelty buttons, curtain trim, embroidery thread, and silk flowers.

Getting the kids involved in the wedding process will help them be part of the big day. Depending on how many kids, and their ages, consider having a crafts table at the reception where children can do simple projects. —T. O.

Three flower girls (Suzanne's daughters, Madeleine, Caroline, and Olivia Chase), carrying their purses.

KEY

Time: 30 minutes

Technique: basic embellishing, layering, ribbon designs

Level of difficulty: advanced beginner

MATERIALS

Guest book

Red-liner tape, 8" x 10" sheet, 1/4"- and 3/4"-wide rolls

Gold foil flakes (sold for paper-making)

Ribbons of 2 widths

Scrapbooking pearl buckle

Rub-on wedding-related word or quote

Scrapbooking papers, two designs, one for background

A Guest Book to Cherish

designed by Suzanne Chase

Your guest book, visited and signed by each guest, is another wedding detail that can quickly and easily be decorated with scrapbooking supplies. Since you and your spouse will most likely save this item as a wedding keepsake, it makes sense to personalize it in some way. In addition to scrapbooking supplies, gold foil flecks for paper making were pressed into the red-liner tape on our sample, creating a rich gold border.

❋ Cut the background paper to the size of the front cover, and cut the red-liner tape sheet to the size of the front cover as well. Size a smaller rectangle of a complementary paper for the center of the front cover, too, leaving as much border as you wish. Rub on the word or quote on the smaller paper, following the instructions for rub-ons.

❋ To adhere the large background paper to the cover, first apply the trimmed sheet of red-liner tape to the cover. Then peel back the edges of the top liner of the tape, line up the corresponding edges of the paper with the tape's edges, and press the paper into place at the top edge. Slowly peel back the remaining tape liner, pressing the rest of the background paper into place as you go. You can also adhere the background paper with scrap pieces of tape.

❋ To adhere the second, smaller paper rectangle, first cut a rectangle of tape and center it on the large paper on the cover.

Supplies for Guest Book.

❋ Center and attach the smaller paper onto the cover over the red-liner tape rectangle. Then apply a strip of ¼" tape around all the edges. Peel back top liners on tape strips to expose stickiness.

❋ Sprinkle gold foil flecks or glitter over exposed tape strips; then press them into place by swirling them around with your fingertips. A little goes a long way.

❋ Apply a strip of ¾" tape below your quote or word. Peel back its top liner.

❋ Apply a decorative ribbon by adhering it directly onto the tape. Tuck each ribbon end under (approximately ⅛") and press tucked ends into the tape to create no-sew seams.

❋ Layer the ribbons by adhering a ¼" tape strip across the ribbon you just applied to the cover. Adhere a thinner ribbon to the exposed tape. In this instance, a small faux-pearl buckle was threaded through the ribbon before it was applied. Make sure to tuck ribbon ends under.

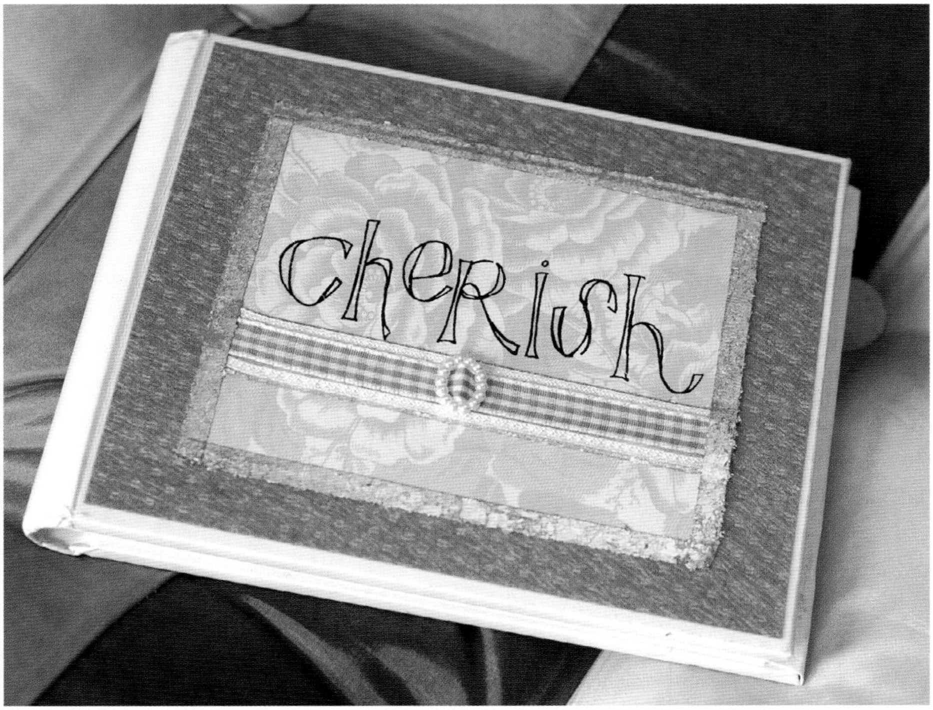

Textured papers, gold foil, and ribbons are layered onto the cover with tape. The word "cherish" is a rub-on, sold for scrapbooking.

Terri O Tips

- *To personalize even further, look for gold-leaf glue pens. You can write with them to personalize and add detail to your special creation.*
- *Cover the rest of your project with the plastic top liner when you are foiling. Foil has a tendency to fly everywhere. Once it sticks, it's stuck.*

FOR FAMILY AND FRIENDS

In this section, we've included projects for and with kids, guys, and pets. Kids are ultrasensitive to the powers of fashion; although they want to fit in, they also want to stand out. You can help them express their unique style by encouraging them to decorate their basic gear. We firmly believe you can jazz up your guy's world a bit, too. Whether his interest is team sports, poker, or fly-fishing, there is a look for him. We've also included a project to dress up your darling pooch.

KEY

Time: 45 minutes

Techniques: ribbon designs, layering

Level of difficulty: beginner

MATERIALS

Backpack

Red-liner tape, ¼"-wide roll and ½" dot roll

Craft glue (optional)

Stickers, ribbons, prestrung sequin trim, silk flowers, rhinestones

Clear glass microbeads or glitter (optional)

Backpack Attack

designed by Suzanne Chase

Your child's backpack is her main accessory throughout the school year. Because they come in so many shapes, sizes, and colors, backpacks are perfect for embellishing. Your daughter can add her school letters and colors, or jazz it up with pictures of her friends or a favorite movie star. Let her dig into your cache of goodies as well as her own, and have her decorate to her heart's content.

❋ Apply strips of red-liner tape along the seams of the backpack. You can also decorate along the zipper lines. Peel back the tape's top liner to expose the sticky tape. *Note:* If you think the backpack will get a lot of wear and tear, use craft glue instead of red-liner tape.

Supplies for decorated backpack.

✳ Decorate seams with ribbons. Here, ¼" ribbon was zigzagged.

✳ To layer ribbon, add a strip of ⅛" tape on top of the zigzagged ribbon and apply another ribbon or trim.

✳ On our model, prestrung sequins were applied. For added interest, use other embellishments, too. We used small dots to apply coated vellum and plastic stickers, as well as rhinestones and flowers designed for scrapbooking and paper crafts.

✳ If any exposed tape remains once you are done embellishing, place the backpack in a shallow pan and pour microbeads or glitter over these areas to cover. Tap backpack on side to remove excess beads.

Backpack decorated with stickers, appliqués, rhinestones, and ribbons.

Time: up to 30 minutes

Technique: basic embellishing, ribbon designs

Level of difficulty: beginner

MATERIALS

Ruler

Red-liner tape, 1" wide

Craft glue (optional)

Thin ribbon trim

Clear glass microbeads, glitter, or colored sand

Novelty buttons, star-shaped

Faux jewelry cabochons

We'll try anything if it means they'll do their homework. —T. O.

Jazzy Rulers

designed by Suzanne Chase

Your kids will love decorating their rulers with novelty buttons, rhinestones, and other goodies. They can also decorate their pens, markers, pencil cases, and sharpeners. The sky's the limit. These decorated items make great gifts for teachers, too.

❊ Apply a strip of 1"-wide tape down the center of the ruler. Peel back the tape's protective liner to expose its stickiness.

❊ Adhere embellishments to your liking. Here, star-shaped novelty buttons were adhered to the ruler and then a tricolor scrapbooking trim was zigzagged in between the buttons. A second ruler was embellished with assorted faux jewels.

❊ Once the decorating is complete, place the ruler in a shallow pan and pour beads, glitter, or colored sand over any remaining exposed tape to fully cover. Tap project on its side to dislodge loose materials.

Note: For a more permanent ruler, use a strong craft glue instead of red-liner tape. This is particularly important for small children.

Supplies for Jazzy Rulers.

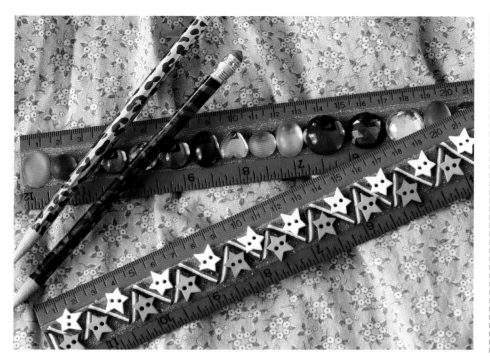

Iridescent cabochons and novelty buttons were used to perk up school rulers.

Terri O Tips

• Buttons, faux jewels, and rhinestones are perfect embellishments. To find items small enough for this project, look in the scrap-booking aisle.

• If you want to jazz up something that you use a lot, it's best to keep big and bulky embellishments to a minimum; they might just get in the way.

Attractive Retainer Case

designed by Suzanne Chase

KEY

Time: 30 minutes

Technique: basic embellishing

Level of difficulty: beginner

MATERIALS

Plastic retainer case

Red-liner tape, 4" x 6" (or larger) sheet

Embellishments from half-used kid's activity kits you may have tucked away at home, e.g., sequins, polymer clay beads, confetti, rhinestones

Colored sand

Pencil

Braces have become quite fashionable now that sparkle and glow-in-the-dark retainers are available, as well as a rainbow assortment of O-rings in custom colors. We encourage you to add more fashion to your child's smile by sprucing up her retainer case with the remains of a half-used activity kit or two.

✳ Trace the retainer case shape onto the paper side of a red-liner tape sheet, and cut out. Adhere the tape to top of retainer case by peeling off tape's backing and pressing gently into place. Then peel back tape's top liner to expose its stickiness.

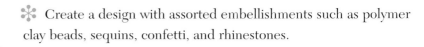

❉ Create a design with assorted embellishments such as polymer clay beads, sequins, confetti, and rhinestones.

❉ When you are pleased with your design, place the container in a shallow pan and pour colored sand over any remaining exposed tape to fully cover it. Tap off excess.

Supplies for attractive retainers.

Leftovers from a child's activity kit were perfect for embellishing this retainer case.

Having a container like this makes wearing a retainer a little more bearable.

Here's another idea: Your child can put her favorite pop star, athlete, or pet on the cover (see Enhancing Images, on page 30). —T. O.

Styling Together

designed by Susan Zimmerman

KEY

Time: 30 minutes

Techniques: thread effects, trimming

Level of difficulty: beginner

MATERIALS

Child's basic jeans and child's top that coordinate with her doll's jeans and top

Red-liner tape, ¾"- and ¼"-wide rolls

Thin decorative braid

Beaded trim with sequins

Small floral appliques

Ricrac

Clear glass microbeads

Fabric transfer sheets for printer, such as June Tailor Printer Fabric Colorfast Quick Fuse™ (optional)

Photo (optional)

Fancy up doll clothes and accessories by embellishing them. Better yet, create matching outfits for your little one and her doll by adding decorative trim to both her jeans and her doll's jeans. You can launder the jeans in your dryer using one of those home dry cleaning systems, sold in grocery stores, or simply pull trim off and reapply when jeans are clean. This will work a couple of times before the tape loses its sticking power.

❋ Apply appropriate-sized red-liner tape around the waistband of the child's jeans as well as around the waistband of her doll's jeans. Apply tape along the pocket edges and on the inside of the pants hem, too. Peel back the top liner of each area's tape as you go.

❋ Apply beaded fringe with sequins to the pants cuffs by adhering the trim to the inside of the hem and letting the beaded part hang down.

Fabric trim was applied with strips of tape to jazz up these denim doll's pants.

Maybe this is how Vera Wang began. —T. O.

Here, the doll's T-shirt is adorned with a photo of her owner.

It seems the boys always get left out when it comes to crafts. This project proves that boys can express themselves, too. —T.O.

✳ Use scrapbook fibers such as ricrac to embellish the doll's waistband.

✳ Adhere sequined clothing trim in rows over the entire waistband of the child's jeans.

✳ Use a decorative flower appliqué in a coordinating color to embellish the jeans snap.

✳ Draw thread designs onto the pocket seams by guiding the braid with one hand while pressing it in place with the other.

✳ Place the embellished area of jeans in a shallow container, and pour micro-beads or glitter over any remaining exposed red-liner tape to fully cover tape.

✳ Optional: Create coordinating T-shirts for your daughter and dolly by printing out photos of your child onto fabric transfer sheets (see Image Transfer, page 29). Size each photo to fit the shirt it will adorn. Tape the images to the shirts with red-liner tape, and decorate around them with ricrac and faux flowers.

Go-Team Binder

designed by Terri O

Since notebooks, like backpacks, are carried around at school all day long, they become another canvas on which kids can express themselves. Boys will welcome the opportunity to communicate their interests, if you supply them with themed embellishments to match them. Here, a football theme is created with textured papers, scrapbooking tokens, and a star punch.

✳ Cut a football shape (a large oval) out of tan paper by using a cutting template or by tracing an item of the same shape. Next, cut your goalposts out of a complementary paper (here, a paper made from metal fibers was used for its texture). The top edges were cut on the bias.

✳ Cut textured star shapes out of a faux-pigskin paper (or any similarly textured paper) using a cutter punch.

KEY

Time: 1 hour

Technique: paper mosaics; layering; thread designs

Level of difficulty: advanced beginner

MATERIALS

Notebook

Red-liner tape, 8 x10 sheet, 1"-wide roll, and 1/2" dots

Textured papers, including tan, brown, and gray

Star-shaped cutter punch

Letter tokens

Novelty buttons, star-shaped

Dimensional embroidery threads in tan

Clear glass microbeads

Pencil

Novelty buttons, textured scrapbook papers, and a cutter punch helped to create this football-themed notebook cover.

✳ Adhere goalposts to notebook's cover by applying 1" tape along each side of the notebook's front cover and pressing the goalposts onto the exposed tape.

✳ Next, apply a sheet of red-liner tape over the football and trim it to size. Apply strips of tape to the back of the football, and tack the football into place by pressing it firmly onto the notebook. Peel back the red-liner tape's top liner on football shape to expose its stickiness.

✳ Decorate football with textured paper stars by pressing them into the tape.

✳ When you are pleased with your design, place notebook cover in a shallow pan and pour microbeads over any remaining exposed tape to fully cover. Tap project on its side to dislodge excess beads.

✳ Apply ¼" tape near each end of the football and adhere a strip of star-shaped novelty buttons to the exposed tape (see photo). Apply a 2"-long strip

KEY

Time: 1 hour

Technique: image embellishing

Level of difficulty: intermediate

MATERIALS

Looseleaf binder

Artwork image, copied and trimmed to size

Red-liner tape, 8" x 10" sheet and ¾"-wide roll

Scrapbook paper for background

¼"-wide checked ribbon

Dimensional embroidery thread

Ricrac

Scrapbooking fiber assortment for writing name

Clear glass microbeads

of 1"-wide tape to the center of the football, peel back the top liner, and add crisscrossed dimensional embroidery threads to create the sewn seam.

✳ Apply letter tokens and other novelty buttons to the cover with ½" tape dots.

Closeup of star-punched paper.

Fall Looseleaf Binder

designed by Suzanne Chase

A watercolor of autumn leaves by my daughter was so spectacular that I was inspired to use it to dress up her looseleaf binder. I enhanced it with embroidery threads and added to the design with coordinating scrapbook papers and ribbons.

✳ Tack scrapbook paper, trimmed to size, to the cover of the looseleaf binder with strips of ¾" red-liner tape. (This is a great time to use tape scraps.) Next, center the artwork image over the papered cover and tack that into place with additional strips or scraps of red-liner tape.

✳ Apply a sheet of tape over the scrapbook paper background and artwork to cover it entirely. This is done by peeling the backing off the top edges of the tape sheet, lining up the exposed tape edges with the edges of the looseleaf binder, and pressing them gently into place. Then slowly peel the rest of the backing off the tape sheet, pressing the tape onto the image as you go.

✿ Smooth out tape with fingertips. Frame the taped image with additional tape to finish covering the top of the looseleaf binder. Peel back all top tape liners to expose sticky tape.

✿ Smoosh ¼" ribbon around the borders of the looseleaf binder (see page 23 for Smooshing). Next, outline the artwork images (in this case, the leaves) with embroidery threads. This is done by guiding the threads with one hand while pressing them into place with the other. Here, Caroline's name was written free-hand with scrapbooking fibers. A ricrac trim was applied to frame the artwork. To secure your threadwork, replace the top protective liner over the exposed tape and press threads firmly into the tape before going on to the next step.

✿ Place looseleaf binder in a shallow container and pour clear glass microbeads over any remaining exposed tape areas to fully cover them. The clearness of the beads allows the artwork and paper pattern to show through, but adds a 3-D effect.

My daughter Caroline's artwork, which was the foundation of the design.

Terri O Tips

• *Use a brayer or credit card to smooth out tape over the image.*

• *If you don't like the way your thread writing is coming out, you can always pull it off and try again.*

The artwork, covered in beads and threads, is the focal point of this colorful looseleaf binder.

*Bits of Dad's old ties and
buttons from his clothing are
used to decorate this leather
frame. Embroidery thread adds
additional texture.*

Daddy's Natty Frame

designed by Suzanne Chase

*Dads never seem to have enough pictures for the office, so picture frames
make an excellent gift. The kids can help decorate this clever frame by
adhering bits and pieces of old ties, denim, and buttons to it. The leather
frame used here was purchased quite inexpensively at a discount store. Once
you have done one, you probably will think of friends or other family members who would enjoy a frame also.*

✻ Adhere red-liner tape strips around the front of the frame. You can cover the whole frame, or leave a bit of it exposed, as was done here. Peel back the tape's top liner to expose its stickiness.

✻ Cut bits of old ties or denim and adhere them to the frame by pressing them into place. Add assorted buttons to design. Curl and coil decorative metallic threads in all the remaining nooks and crannies.

✻ When you are pleased with your design, place the frame in a shallow container and pour microbeads over any remaining exposed tape. Swirl beads with fingertips to fully cover. Tap project on its side to dislodge excess beads.

✻ Necktie fabric can be used to decorate an eyeglass case as well.

An eyeglass case can be jazzed up with bits of fabric and scrapbooking tiles.

Terri O Tips

• Scraps from other clothing would work well, too: flannel shirts, dress shirts, patterned boxers or pajamas, etc.

• Why not buy an inexpensive tie and customize it? With red-liner tape, you can add a fun appliqué for any event. Use it, then lose it.

• Your man may like to see his name on something. It's easy to do and easy to remove.

Poker-Face Portfolio

designed by Terri O

Poker cards and chips, combined with scrapbook lettering and ribbon, create this playful portfolio cover.

Although men aren't big on embellished items, they will embrace certain themes as long as they are tastefully done. The ever-popular game of poker is a good choice for many. The game pieces are good to use for embellishing, since they have a flat surface to adhere to the tape. The portfolio shown here uses actual poker chips, along with scrapbooking embellishments.

❋ The cards are decorated first and then adhered to the portfolio. Cover each playing card with a red-liner tape sheet, trimmed to size. To do this, peel the backing off one end of the tape sheet and line it up with the corresponding edges of the playing card. Press the tape edges onto the edges of the image. Then slowly peel the rest of the backing off the tape sheet, pressing the tape onto the image as you go, until it is completely covered. Peel back the tape's protective liner to expose its stickiness.

❋ Use ⅛" ribbon to frame the cards. Create a zigzag pattern on one card, and put strips on the other.

❋ Use embroidery thread to outline details of the playing card images. This is where those curved tweezers come in real handy. When dealing with such intricate designs, they help you adhere the thread and twist and turn with the curves of the design.

❋ Once the embellishing is done, place the cards in a shallow pan and pour clear microbeads over any remaining exposed tape to fully cover it.

❋ Tack the cards onto the portfolio cover with scrap tape.

❋ Apply sticker lettering directly onto the portfolio cover and onto the poker chips. Then adhere the poker chips to the cover with ½" tape dots. Some poker chips, as well as some other items you may use, will require a double layer of tape because each chip has a depression in the center. It's better to be safe than sorry.

Closeup of an embroidered playing card.

Terri O Tips

• When creating for your man, use items from his hobby or his work.

• Other potential themes include golf, bowling, fishing, hunting, sports, wine, music, and junk food.

• Company logos and business cards are perfect embellishments.

Time: up to 1 hour

Techniques: image embellishing, paper mosaics, layering, thread effects

Level of difficulty: advanced beginner

MATERIALS

Nail kit

Duck motif rub-on

Red-liner tape, 4" x 6" sheet and ½" dots

Wallpaper scraps or other decorative papers

Clear plastic magnifying page pebbles (scrapbook supply)

Sticker letters

Dimensional embroidery thread

Yarn

Clear glass microbeads

> I have stacks of wallpaper books and samples. You never know when they might come in handy! —T. O.

Outdoorsy Nail Kit

designed by Terri O

The nail kit sports a duck motif, which came from a set of rub-on transfers. The image was embellished with thread and yarn, creating an embroidered look. Scrapbook lettering and clear plastic magnifying pebbles were used to create the monogram.

The finished Nail Kit.

✳ Apply the duck rub-ons to cover of nail kit, following the directions given for rub-ons. The nail kit used here has a fabric cover, so it was a bit more challenging to apply the rub-on because of the texture. Heavily textured surfaces are even more difficult. As with any rub-on, make sure your surface is really clean before you begin.

✳ Trim a sheet of red-liner tape to fit over the rub-on image and adhere the tape to the nail kit. To do this, peel the backing off one end of the tape sheet and line it up with the area you want to cover on the nail kit. Press the tape edges onto the cover of the kit. Then slowly peel the rest of the backing off the tape sheet, pressing the tape onto the rub-on image as you go, until it is completely covered.

✳ Outline the rub-on image (we used ducks) in dimensional embroidery thread. This is done by guiding the threads with one hand while pressing them into place with the other. (Once again, those tweezers will come in real handy.)

✳ Zigzag textured yarn around the border of the duck image to frame it.

✳ Trim another piece of tape for the initials nameplate and adhere tape to the portfolio. Then peel back the tape's top liner to expose its stickiness.

✳ To create the "monogram," tear decorative papers and press onto the tape. Apply sticker letters over the paper collage. Adhere clear plastic pebbles over the sticker lettering, using ½" tape dots.

✳ When the design work is completed, place the nail kit in a shallow container and pour clear microbeads over it to fill in any remaining exposed tape areas.

Rub-on transfers.

KEY

Time: 20 minutes

Techniques: basic embellishing, wrapping, layering

Level of difficulty: advanced beginner

MATERIALS

Dog collars and leash

Red-liner tape, ¾"-wide roll

Strong craft glue

¾"-wide ribbons

Red chenille yarn

Novelty themed buttons

Clear glass microbeads (if you use tape)

Small plastic mirror tiles

Collars can be decorated for every occasion using odds and ends from scrapbooking, sewing, and knitting.

Festive Collars

designed by Suzanne Chase

Your pet can dress for any fancy occasion if you make her an embellished collar or leash. Four samples are given here. In one example shown, our dog is getting all dressed up in a floral collar for her spring birthday party. The pup in another photo is ready for a Christmas gathering. Wrapped collars and leashes are quick and easy to decorate; you can change the look for any and all special events in minutes. Note: If you have an active animal, we recommend gluing any small decorations on with a strong craft glue so they cannot be knocked or scratched off and eaten by your pet.

Mirror-Tiled Collar

✳ Apply a strip of red-liner tape to cover entire length of collar exterior, excluding the part with the holes. Peel back tape's protective liner to expose its stickiness. (Use glue instead of tape for a more permanent attachment.)

✳ Decorate collar with mirror tiles in desired pattern by pressing them lightly into place.

❄ Place collar in a shallow dish and pour clear glass microbeads over any remaining exposed tape to fully cover (if you used tape). Gently press beads into place with your fingers. Tap collar on its side to dislodge excess beads.

Red Chenille Leash

❄ Apply a strip of red-liner tape lengthwise to the underside of the leash. Then peel back top protective liner to expose sticky tape.

❄ Starting on the underside of the leash at one end, wrap chenille yarn around and around until the whole leash is covered in yarn. The exposed tape will hold the yarn in place each time you wrap. When you have finished, trim off excess yarn ends, turn them under, and press them firmly into place.

Floral Leash and Christmas Collar

❄ Follow instructions for wrapping given with the Red Chenille Leash, but use ribbon instead of yarn.

❄ Apply decorative buttons or flowers by adhering them to the wrapped collar or leash with scraps of red-liner tape. Use button shank remover if needed. For an active dog, use strong craft glue instead for a more permanent hold.

Cody the cockapoo is wearing his holiday collar, created by wrapping festive ribbon around a plain collar. Holiday novelty buttons were adhered to the ribbon (left).

Maxine's collar and leash were wrapped in ribbon and then embellished with silk flowers for her springtime birthday (far left).

Metric Chart

Inches to Millimeters
and Centimeters

Inches	MM	CM
⅛	3	0.3
¼	6	0.6
⅜	10	1.0
½	13	1.3
⅝	16	1.6
¾	19	1.9
⅞	22	2.2
1	25	2.5
1¼	32	3.2
1½	38	3.8
1¾	44	4.4
2	51	5.1
2½	64	6.4
3	76	7.6
3½	89	8.9
4	102	10.2
4½	114	11.4
5	127	12.7
6	152	15.2
7	178	17.8
8	203	20.3
9	229	22.9
10	254	25.4
11	279	27.9
12	305	30.5
13	330	33.0
14	356	35.6
15	381	38.1

MM=Millimeters CM=Centimeters

Acknowledgments

A big thanks to Terri O for recognizing the excitement of crafting with red-liner Treasure Tape™ and for joining us to spread the word. Thanks to Jerry Zimmerman, photographer extraordinaire, who has brought our passion to life with his gorgeous photography. No less important is my business partner, Susan Zimmerman, for her undying enthusiasm as well as her substantial contribution to the projects offered in this book. I also thank Andrew and Doug Kreinik for their commitment to our business and vision. Last but not least, thanks to my husband, Jon, and daughters, Madeleine, Caroline, and Olivia, for believing in me and allowing me to absorb myself in the creation of this book for a few months.

—*Suzanne Chase*

I dedicate this book to my husband, Ray. Without him I certainly would not be where I am today. A big hug and thanks to my kids, Kyle and Tatum, my mom, "Boots," and my business partner, Suzie Guzman, for being there so I can go out and play. And of course, to Sue and Suzanne for thinking just like me!

—*Terri O*

Additionally, we thank those companies and people who contributed products for the projects created in the book, including: Kreinik, EK Success, Etal Metal Fiber Papers, Doodlebug Designs, Junkitz, Michael Miller Fabrics, Lil Davis, May Arts, Offray Ribbon, Prima Marketing, Wimpole Street, Making Memories, Sandtastik, Jewelcraft, Art Institute Glitter, Anna Griffin, Paper Fever, June Tailor, Blumenthal Lansing, Undu, Fiskars, Bazzill Papers, Fibermark, Bagworks, Trimtex, and JHB Buttons. Thanks also to Christina Santangelo for her project contributions and for the loan of the wonderful textiles we used for styling some of our shots. Last, but not least, thank you to Jo Fagan and Isabel Stein for guiding the publication of this book.

Index

About the Authors

Author Suzanne Chase is co-owner of Treasure Tape™, a brand of extra-strength, double-sided red-liner tape sold in the craft industry (see www.treasuretape.com). She and her partner, Susan Zimmerman, who also contributed to the book with project designs, are innovators of red-liner tape crafting and are known in the industry for their leading-edge techniques and ideas. To date, they have designed and written *Instant Paper Treasures*, a project book on paper crafts created with red-liner tape. Suzanne and Sue have appeared on national television, on HGTV, DIY, and QVC, to demonstrate their exciting world of instant embellishing. In addition, they have designed and written up project ideas for popular consumer craft magazines including *Creating Keepsakes*, *Home Arts*, *Memories Community*, and *Beyond Scrapbooking*. Suzanne and Sue each have three daughters, including a set of twins each.

Terri O, originally crowned the "Craft Queen" some 15 years ago, is the reigning national spokesperson for the Craft and Hobby Association. Terri regularly appears on morning shows across the country as well as on shows on HGTV, The Discovery Channel, and QVC, spreading her message of creativity. With a background in television news as an anchor and as a specialty features correspondent, Terri turned to crafts to keep her sanity in the face of all of the bad news she had to report. Terri O became the media darling of news not only for her skills as a journalist but because she could transition into the Craft Queen every morning on "Good Morning Arizona." Currently, she is the host of her own show, "On the Go with Terri O," which specializes in projects for those of us with busy lifestyles. Terri has two young boys, and has plans for her own national TV show.